W9-BFE-993

FIGURES OF CATASTROPHE

FIGURES OF CATASTROPHE

The Condition of Culture Novel

FRANCIS MULHERN

VERSO
London • New York

First published by Verso 2016

1 3 5 7 9 10 8 6 4 2

Verso
UK: 6 Meard Street, London W1F 0EG
US: 20 Jay Street, Suite 1010, Brooklyn, NY 11201
www.versobooks.com

Verso is the imprint of New Left Books

ISBN-13: 978-1-78478-191-0 (HB)
eISBN-13: 978-1-78478-193-4 (US)
eISBN-13: 978-1-78478-194-1 (UK)

British Library Cataloguing in Publication Data
A catalogue record for this book is available from the British Library

Library of Congress Cataloging-in-Publication Data

Mulhern, Francis.
 Figures of catastrophe : the condition of culture novel
/ Francis Mulhern.
    pages cm
 Includes bibliographical references and index.
 ISBN 978-1-78478-191-0 (hardback)
 1. English fiction–20th century–History and criticism.
 2. Literature and society–England–History–20th
century. 3. Labor movement in literature. 4. Working
class in literature. I. Title.
 PR888.L3M85 2015
 823'.91093520623–dc23
                    2015028002

Typeset in Fournier by MJ & N Gavan, Truro, Cornwall
Printed and bound by CPI Group (UK) Ltd, Croydon, CR0 4YY

Contents

Preface

This book had its effective beginning in an invitation to teach for a semester in the English Department at Johns Hopkins University. But its basic conception lies further back in time. Nearly forty years ago, I wrote *The Moment of 'Scrutiny'*, a book that attempted to reconstruct the history of a highly charged passage in twentieth-century cultural criticism. Out of a sentence or two in its closing pages, years later, came a second book, *Culture/Metaculture*, a general critique of cultural criticism and its successor formation, cultural studies. Here, now, is another marsupial birth, this one germinated in the course of a critical exchange over *Metaculture* in which it came to me that the literary self-representations of 'culture' – a few novels immediately suggested themselves – told a darker story than anything to be found in the record of cultural criticism proper, with its defining commitments to the great powers of form and idea, or what Matthew Arnold termed 'sweetness and light'. Thus, after further years of work, including some big surprises, the initial opportunity afforded by Hopkins has led to *Figures of Catastrophe*, the third part of an unplanned, informal trio offering elements of a critical history of metaculture, the discourse in which the principle of 'culture' speaks of itself and its general conditions of existence.

Fundamental matters of theory are involved here. Nevertheless, as one friendly reader has pointed out, this is a book that does without any more or less elaborate preamble concerning theory or method. He was not suggesting that there was an omission to be made good. But a few opening indications may not go amiss. This is an essay in Marxist formalism, the noun emphasizing the making of meaning as the proper object of literary study, the modifier marking off an orientation in historical understanding and a political commitment. In a way it is full of theory, years' worth of it, as presupposition or implication or simple trace of reading, and from time to time as explicit citation. But my leading purpose here is not theoretical, even if an attempt to clarify and illustrate the scope and potential of a certain understanding of 'genre' gives the work its conceptual accent. Its main mode is literary-historical, and my hope is that the Introduction provides as much preliminary discussion as will be needed.

This is a book about novels, and specifically the genre I call 'the condition of culture novel' – or rather, a group of novels I take to instantiate what I take to be a genre. My pedantic phrasing has a point. Neither the group – as the novels now are – nor the ascription was pre-given. They and it emerged in a dialectic that remains unfinished, leaving all conclusions provisional. The group is largely 'literary' in character, belonging to the overlapping canons of academia and polite journalism, and I cannot say what there may be to find in a developed international comparison, not to speak of the great expanses of unashamed 'genre' writing, or the marginal, oppositional initiatives of avant-gardes: only that there will certainly be something, and that it seems unlikely that my general characterizations will emerge unqualified from new encounters in those cultural registers. Others will report in due time.

Author's acknowledgements, especially those of academic provenance, seem more and more drawn to self-promoting or maudlin excursions in life-writing. I hope to avoid these embarrassments while not scanting my debts. Looking back on the semester at Hopkins and the English graduate seminar in which this book originated, I am reminded of what I owe to Amanda Anderson, Simon During, Frances Ferguson, Christiane Gannon, Susie Hermann, Rob Higney, Kevin Lenfest, Beth Steedley and Karen Tiefenwerth. My thanks to them all.

For a timely provocation I owe a particular debt to Stefan Collini.

Perry Anderson, Franco Moretti, Peter Osborne and Susan Watkins all made valuable criticisms and suggestions, to which I hope I have done some justice.

Rachel Malik's critical advice and support were crucial throughout.

Introduction to a Genre

The aim of this short study is to uncover the topics and forms of an unnoticed genre in English writing since the 1890s: the condition of culture novel. This wording is ungainly, it is true. My plea of justification is that, in its emphatic recall of Thomas Carlyle's famous phrase, 'the condition of England',[1] it captures both the formative associations of the genre and its specific difference from them. In keeping with the great tradition of cultural criticism to which Carlyle belongs, the work of the condition of culture novel is one of synoptic evaluation: its vocation is to frame and assess *the whole*, however that may be conceived. However, this whole is not the social totality. The elective emphasis of the genre is the plane of culture, the social order of meanings and values, and the institutions and practices by which, specifically, these are formed and circulated. This double demarcation governs the selection of novels I discuss here. Synopticism alone would not be sufficient

---

1   The opening words of his *Past and Present* (1843).

to uphold a distinction between this genre, with its constitutive emphasis on culture, and the broader, and much older, tradition of social realism of which it is, perhaps, no more than a subset. But it does, nevertheless, dictate a principle of selection in the miscellaneous generality of novels about culture. Novels such as George Gissing's *New Grub Street* (1891), Somerset Maugham's *Cakes and Ale* (1930), Evelyn Waugh's *Scoop* (1938) and Murray Sayle's *A Crooked Sixpence* (1960) are in their different ways notable critical treatments of literature and journalism in their time, but they are all more or less specialized in focus, not synoptic. The same can be said about Kingsley Amis's *Lucky Jim* (1954), Angus Wilson's *Anglo-Saxon Attitudes* (1956) or Malcolm Bradbury's *The History Man* (1975) as novels with a focus in the university. The distinctive character of the condition of culture novel is that it is both synoptic and specific, foregrounding the cultural dimension of the social whole, undertaking a synoptic narrative evaluation of the social relations of culture.

My detailed discussions range across more than a dozen novels, and at least as many more make brief appearances. It may make for an easier passage through these introductory remarks if the primary texts are identified now, in order of treatment and grouped according to the four main chapters of the book:

Thomas Hardy, *Jude the Obscure*, 1896
E.M. Forster, *Howards End*, 1910

Virginia Woolf, *Orlando*, 1928
————, *Between the Acts*, 1941
Evelyn Waugh, *Brideshead Revisited*, 1945

Elizabeth Bowen, *The Heat of the Day*, 1948
Stan Barstow, *A Kind of Loving*, 1960

John Fowles, *The Collector*, 1963
Ruth Rendell, *A Judgement in Stone*, 1977

Martin Amis, *Money*, 1984
V.S. Naipaul, *The Enigma of Arrival*, 1987
———, *The Mimic Men*, 1967
Hanif Kureishi, *The Black Album*, 1995
Zadie Smith, *On Beauty*, 2005

My understanding of *genre* calls for some comment – as does any use of that term, indeed, since the word can be found at every level of discrimination of literary kinds.[2] It has been used to denominate the basic *formats of enunciation*, the ancient epic (narrative) and dramatic, and their adoptive modern sibling, the lyric – or more confusingly, to denominate some but not all of them. The status of genre is more often awarded to the great trans-historical evaluative *modes*, which are ontological in suggestion, notably Northrop Frye's *mythoi*, tragedy, comedy, romance and satire, and others, such as pastoral and the fantastic – or again, and again confusingly, to some but not all of them.[3] At a lower and more appropriate level of classification, the term is routinely called upon to distinguish high from low literary registers: it circulates widely as a designator for popular narrative varieties

2   For a conspectus, see David Duff, ed., *Modern Genre Theory*, Harlow, 2000. John Frow's *Genre* (London: 2005) is an exceptionally interesting recent theoretical statement.

3   Northrop Frye, *Anatomy of Criticism* (1957), Princeton, 1971, pp. 131–9.

such as crime, romance and fantasy, but with the mystifying suggestion that polite writing, 'the literary novel', being 'serious', is exempt from the reductive formulas of mere 'genre'. Indeed it is not, and cannot be. The concept of genre, as I understand it, in the broad traditions of Georg Lukács and Mikhail Bakhtin, applies at a relatively low level of historical generality, identifying groups of texts sharing a distinctive topic or set of topics. The distinctive topic of the *Bildungsroman*, to take an uncontroversial (and directly relevant) instance, is growing up and into a social world. That is what unites *Emma* (1815) and *The Confusions of Young Törless* (1906), *Le Rouge et le noir* (1830) and *Tess of the d'Urbervilles* (1891), for all their deep individuality. At the same time, however, the tropology of the *Bildungsroman*, its store of situations and sequences, is everywhere in modern narrative culture, far exceeding the recognizable boundaries of the genre proper, and this observable fact illustrates a fundamental implication of the concept of genre: it is not so much a classification as a formative power, a force of literary production. Or as Raymond Williams would say, in glossing his own related idea of 'convention', it is 'a way of seeing'.[4]

Genre is ubiquitous, a fundamental condition of all intelligible utterance, literary and other. Contrary to the limiting suggestion of the stock phrase 'genre fiction', it can accommodate great and significant variation from one practitioner to another, from one text to another. This is in large measure because the empirical textual reality of genre is very often plural. In assigning a novel to a genre, we are usually naming its generic dominant, not an essence that saturates it; many texts belong to more than

---

4   Raymond Williams, *The Long Revolution* (1961), Harmondsworth, 1965.

one genre. Another Gissing novel, *In the Year of Jubilee* (1894), offers a pertinent case in point. It is, in the first place, a *Zeitroman* or novel of the times, a conspectus of London middle-class life in the late 1880s, and within this frame the matter of culture and education is prominent. Suburbanization and the quickening consumer economy are strong themes; the book is memorable for its foregrounding of advertising as a defining social and cultural relationship – and the term 'culture' is itself central in the vocabulary of the novel, as a pejorative term commonly suggesting vain or fraudulent pretension in its producers and users alike, something little more than an instrumental resource in a field of rivalrous social aspiration. Thus, *In the Year of Jubilee* can also be thought of as a condition of culture novel. However, the narrative stake throughout is marriageability, the matching and mismatching of eros, money and social status in the lives of women with aspirations to independence. Gissing's novel is above all an example (a signally misogynistic example) of so-called New Woman fiction. Of the novels discussed in the following chapters, some five or six are *Bildungsromane* of sorts, and two of these – *Jude the Obscure* and *Brideshead Revisited* – share the further distinction of modulating into novels of adultery, both of which in their turn close on the narrative trope of female renunciation. *On Beauty* is among other things a campus novel, itself a latter-day variation on the perdurable genre of Menippean satire, concerning the follies of learned men (and women). It is, accordingly, relatively specialized in cultural focus, but has been included here in virtue of its explicit dialogic affiliation with *Howards End*, the indisputable keystone of the English genre. Unlikely parallels coexist with startling variety. The modal repertoire of these and the other novels I discuss is wide, including tragedy, comedy, pastoral and satire, and several varieties of the fantastic, including horror. In ontological suggestion they range from the realist through the twilight zones of romance and the uncanny to the plainly marvellous. All, in their individual ways, are instances of the condition of culture novel.

Dominant in these cases, the topics of the condition of culture novel can also appear in subordinate, or secondary, narrative roles, with the result that the core texts are surrounded, in the real world of writing, by others whose affinities may be evident, and sometimes arresting, but not in the end sufficiently concentrated or sustained to warrant their assignment to the genre. *In the Year of Jubilee* is one such. Another is Graham Greene's *Stamboul Train* (1932), a novel written in the shadow of T. S. Eliot's poetic cultural criticism – so I would say – but not in shadow so deep as to give the work its final character. Bowen's *The Heat of the Day* (1948), although not a condition of culture novel either, offers, in the person of Louie, a latter-day new woman to sit with Gissing's specimens, and a classic figuration of the heteronomous reading subject, the stock life form of F.R. Leavis's 'mass civilization'. (This, along with Smith's novel, was a borderline case I could not set aside.) Such instances are important for what they show of the social reality of genre as a force of production. A truly telling visualization of genre, in contrast with Linnaeus's and Mendeleev's tables, would have to be animated. Always already formed or in formation, genres are trans-textual, inscribed across texts, sometimes shaping them decisively, at other times inflecting them, contributing to more complex outcomes. They are historically formed ways of seeing.

*   *   *

The general way of seeing to which the condition of culture novel in its turn belongs is what I have elsewhere termed 'metacultural discourse', or simply 'metaculture': a discourse in which culture reflects on its own generality and conditions of existence.[5] This discourse is invariably critical, and in its main, classic form of cultural criticism, tends strongly, though not exclusively, towards pessimism and an abstracted conservatism. Metacultural discourse is propelled by the conviction that culture, in its concrete historical existence, is inadequate to the norms implied in its essential endowment of value, in the cultural principle.[6] This principle, whatever its content may be taken to be in any given instance, is the vantage-point of critical observation, the subject-position of metacultural discourse, from which it scrutinizes the bad object-culture of the times. That culture, or 'civilization' as it has often been termed, with strict limiting implication, may be that of industrialism or political democracy or even capitalism. In any case, it systematically obstructs the full exercise of cultural capabilities and threatens perhaps to dissipate them altogether.

The thematic commitments of cultural criticism remain notably consistent over time: a louring modernity and a threatened cause are the poles of the common narrative. The condition of culture novel is more resistant to generalization. This is in part because the texts are novels committed to miming phenomenal worlds according to shared norms of observation, fictions whose lexicons and repertoires of situation and event are strongly individual, and hardly less so just because critical comparison, with its controlled perversity of attention, claims to discover strong

---

5   See my *Culture/Metaculture*, London, 2000.

6   Compare Theodor Adorno, 'Cultural Criticism and Society', *Prisms*, London, 1967, pp. 19–20.

patterns. Even within the framing commitment of a synoptic evaluation of cultural relations, there is much diversity. The cultural principle itself is a shape-shifter, appearing variously as nationality or vocation, a sculpture or a tree, a house or a manner of writing. Some of the novels are written in conscious affiliation to metacultural tradition: *Howards End* is a deliberate work of Arnoldian revisionism, and, a century later, Zadie Smith looked to that novel as an inspiration and a resource for *On Beauty*. Others are the more remarkable for showing no awareness of their discursive kinship. The entire inventory of English cultural criticism is on display in these novels: flats, suburbs, motor-cars, advertising, television and unread books. But so too is the trope of the past as burden and blockage – not a thought to gladden an Eliot or a Leavis. Every modality of cultural desire finds expression, in more or less intense degree, including, at the limit, the desire to have nothing to do with 'culture'. High culture appears in its various postures as mission, prophecy, criticism, and as dogma, preciousness or property. Set against it, there is simple unculture, an untroubling absence in lives spent by other lights in the social space below. Then there is the dynamic and usually philistine alternative of a commercialized mass culture, and, beyond that, in the later twentieth century, an educated revaluation of pop-cultural hedonism and a considered scepticism towards the high-cultural tradition. Finally, though it is not so much new as newsworthy, in the opening decades of the twenty-first century, there is the challenge of culture as customary difference, often religiously sanctioned, a multiform tendency as severe as any enlightened minority and as demotic as any mass-market populism, and merciless in its condemnation of both.

*   *   *

Nevertheless, these are novels, and only some of what they have to say about their historical worlds and the conflicts that animate them is given directly, in generalizing pronouncements of the kind we expect in the modes of formal argumentation. *The Mimic Men* is rich in aphoristic statements of this kind, and *Howards End* is preceded by a direct ethical plea to readers; *The Black Album* is a sequence of debates. But for much the greater part, the argument – for that is what is always in process, even if the situation is particularized, the manner no more than suggestive, and the suggestions themselves often ambiguous – is implicit in the characters and their situations, the action and its outcomes. In the associative reasoning that is the stuff of novelistic argumentation, fallacy is a resource, not a shortcoming. False disjunctions are commonplace: *Jude the Obscure* notoriously grants young women only two antithetical modes of being: carnality and cunning, or frigid high-mindedness – no third course. In the fallacy *ad hominem*, or device of personalization, a general value is associated with a particular character or characters, contingently, as it were, but in a story whose course and outcomes then suggest a general judgement. Thus, in *Howards End*, the paternity of Helen Schlegel's baby hints at a utopian reconciliation of classes in culture – while the death of the father himself, Leonard Bast, leaves the counter-suggestion (also fallacious) that utopia, a bad utopia, is precisely all it is. The fallacy known as *post hoc ergo propter hoc*, in which the mere fact of sequence appears as a sufficient sign of cause, reinforces the suggestive logic of personalization.[7] Thus, *b* comes after *a*, which therefore is the cause of *b* – and so, a half-century later, the story

---

7   Literally, 'after this, therefore because of this'.

of Fred Clegg, the aspirational pools-winning kidnapper in John Fowles's *The Collector*, points to a darker assessment of working-class cultural desire and potential.

In these respects, the process of cultural evaluation belongs to the plane of diegesis, the narrated world of the novel; in another, it unfolds in the plane of narration, and concerns the distribution of cultural capital between narrator and characters, and between writer and readers. The distinction is of critical importance, illuminating the matter of narrative authority and the means of its consolidation – a defining issue in the condition of culture novel. *The Collector* offers a simple illustration, in Miranda's diary record of a conversation with her captor, Fred (whom she calls Caliban, hence C). He has been talking about his disrupted early years:

M. So your aunt took you over.

C. Yes.

M. Like Mrs Joe and Pip.

C. Who?

M. Never mind.[8]

This is one of many confirmations of the cultural inequality of the two characters. Fred does not recognize Miranda's allusion to *Great Expectations* or even guess that it might be a literary citation rather than a simple real-world reference. However, the narrative does not tell its reader this. On the contrary, it calls for a reader capable of interpreting the conversation correctly, a reader like Miranda, not Clegg. Or perhaps still more capable

---

8   John Fowles, *The Collector* (1963), London, 1989, p. 183.

than Miranda, as it is tempting to infer from her parents' choice of names for their daughters: Miranda and Carmen. The choices suggest refinement – the allusion to *The Tempest* is lost on Clegg. But the conjunction of these borrowings from Shakespeare and Bizet creates a dissonance, summoning up a memory from the upstart cultural registers of Broadway and Hollywood, in the person of the singer and actress Carmen Miranda. In claiming cultural distinction, the Grey parents have blundered into a show of ignorance and pretension. This, so far as we can tell, is lost on Miranda – though not, we may guess, on the likes of her mentor, the artist G.P. And as for the readers making their way through the scheme that Fowles has contrived for them? Narratives of cultural evaluation are necessarily also procedures of cultural qualification. They create their authority in deployments of cultural capital that function to test and (perhaps) confirm their readers as adequate evaluating subjects in their own right. This operation unfolds in the plane of address, and its basic rhetorical form – not unique to the genre, but conspicuously pointed in it – is the tendentious gesture *of course*: the presentation of new knowledge as shared knowledge, of rarefied knowledge as if it were common currency. It is most markedly at work in practices of cultural citation.

Some allusions are so crafted as to make a cryptogram of sorts. The family at the centre of Ruth Rendell's *A Judgement in Stone* bears a name with particular resonance in the history of English literacy and piety (it was a Miles Coverdale who produced the first complete printed translation of the Bible), and in this there is a cryptic accession of meaning that offers the Coverdales not merely as representative of their class, as the narrative does from its first page onwards, but also as historical portents, their lives

and violent deaths figuring a national heritage and its final desolation. Other naming decisions do similar work. Jude, in Catholic
tradition, is the patron saint of hopeless cases. The name Schlegel, in European cultural history, is a legacy in itself. Bast and
Clegg continue a line of monosyllabic surnames suggesting the
hereditary taint of the low-born.[9] The radical pessimism of Hanif
Kureishi's social anthropology, in *The Black Album*, is fixed in the
name of a pub: the Morlock.

That is the extent of the citation. For those who recognize the
reference to H.G. Wells's *Time Machine*, its signification is plain:
the white working class is degenerating into a new, no-longer-
quite-human species. For those who do not, there is nothing even
to suggest that there might be a meaning to elicit – and in that
cultural blankness there may already be a touch of the Morlock.
In one sense, such moments are everywhere in discourse; they
belong to metonymy, one of constitutive axes of language itself,
in which there can never be an ideal fullness of representation.
Nevertheless, part-referencing (as we might relevantly translate
'metonymy') is tendentious when it functions emphatically in the

---

9   The *gg* consonantal form also connotes negatively in English (literary)
proper names, and doubly so in a monosyllable: '*Wragg*!', Matthew Arnold
exclaimed, referring to the case of a workhouse girl accused of infanticide:
'has anyone reflected what a touch of grossness in our race, what an original shortcoming in the more delicate spiritual perceptions, is shown by the
growth amongst us of such hideous names, – Higginbotham, Stiggins, Bugg!
In Ionia and Attica they were luckier …' ('The Function of Criticism at the
Present Time', *Selected Prose*, Harmondsworth, 1970, p. 146). Indeed, Clegg
is thrice accursed. In Scots a *cleg* is a horsefly, a creature on a level with his
own 'bugs'. In another illustration of the power of this phobia, the thrust-
ing literary man in Anthony Powell's novel-sequence *A Dance to the Music of
Time* is marked negatively from the outset, by his Northern origins and even
more so by his surname: Quiggin.

way it does in this genre, as a device indexing qualification and disqualification. Evelyn Waugh's citation of Oxford undergraduate customs makes no concession to readers not already familiar with them. Hardy's scriptural knowledge was less noteworthy in 1895 than it is today, yet even then the appearance of untranslated New Testament Greek must have given pause to many.

The canon of English literature itself is a recurring presence in these novels, in one case – Martin Amis's *Money* – subserving a focused polemical purpose, and in others as an atmosphere or even a co-constituent of the fictional real. Wisps of poetry, normally not attributed and not always clearly associated with a particular character, form one strand in the inter-subjective world of *Between the Acts*.[10] In *A Judgement in Stone*, phrases from Shakespeare, Wordsworth and Keats occur as naturalized elements in the descriptive language of the novel, allusions with a direct denotative value, in a textual economy where literature and landscape are no longer distinct.[11] (The Coverdale family home, Lowfield Hall, itself seems to take its name from the two significant houses in another novel, *Jane Eyre*: Lowood and Thornfield.[12]) Naipaul's *Enigma of Arrival* takes this osmotic tendency to its limit, as the Wiltshire landscapes retune the sensibility that will eventually record them. By means of such

---

10   The poets include, among others, Shakespeare, Shelley, Keats, Byron, Tennyson and Swinburne. In *Howards End*, only a small unmarked fragment of poetry tells the reader that Forster is engaged in a self-aware revaluation of Arnoldian cultural criticism. (See pp. 28–31 below.)

11   Dickens is present too: references to *Bleak House* project the family devastation into a timeless future, which in rhetorical terms is the cultural eternity of the *locus classicus*, the literary byword.

12   Susan Rowland, 'The Spirits of Detection in Women's Crime Fiction', *International Journal of Mythological Studies* 1 (3), 2007, p. 218.

devices, and beyond any particular thematic and stylistic interest they may have, the narrating subject is transfigured. It is English Literature itself that will observe and pass judgement, bringing its overarching authority to bear on the troubling matter of culture.

1. *Imagining Other Lives*

By the end of the nineteenth century, the question of working-class education in Britain was hardly a novelty, however controversial it remained. The principle of universal, publicly supported elementary schooling for children had been established in law for the greater part of a generation. Adults had been served by the Mechanics' Institutes since the 1820s, while the Working Men's Colleges sponsored a liberal arts curriculum from the mid-century onwards. Yet it was now that the topic caught fire in the imaginative field of the English novel, in two stories of working-class educational aspiration that furnished the occasions for general assessments of the current state and prospects of culture. In doing so, Thomas Hardy's *Jude the Obscure* and E. M. Forster's *Howards End* pioneered a new genre, the condition of culture novel. In so far as the aspiration was upheld as legitimate, coherent and sympathetic, these narratives offered social evaluations of a questioning, implicitly radical kind – even though, in truth, the reservations always seemed likely to block the sympathies that sustained the effort of critical imagination against ideological foreclosure. Ambivalence is there already at the heart of the genre's founding classics.

I

Jude the Obscure is a novel full of journeys. Indeed, the journey is the dominant spatial figure of the narrative, taking precedence over place and settlement, as is already manifest in its table of contents, where the principal divisions of the text are named following a simple locative scheme: Marygreen; Christminster; Melchester; Shaston; Aldbrickham and Elsewhere; Christminster Again. This is a list of place-names, each preceded by 'At', a sequence of temporary addresses implying that journeying is the only constant in the matter. The first of these, Marygreen, is already a displacement for the young Jude Fawley: he has arrived there, an orphan by the age of eleven, and his aunt does not know what to do with him. His cousin Sue Bridehead was born there, and is nostalgic for what she remembers as her childhood; but when she returns at last, after the death of her children, it is in an act of moral self-abnegation, and as the novel closes her suffering has not ended. Home, now, is again elsewhere, beyond the grave, with Jude.

The journey that defines the novel – Jude's – is a quest for culture, in three successive forms. It is first of all a desire for the higher learning. Jude, with less than the ordinary elementary schooling but a great appetite for books, decides to follow in the path of his teacher, Phillotson, and prepare himself for the University of Christminster, where he will become a classical scholar. He perseveres in this line of self-education for more than a decade, making his living as a stone-mason, and finally comes to live in Christminster – where his inquiries are ignored or summarily rebuffed. Disheartened, Jude now reformulates his plans: he will pursue 'the ecclesiastic and altruistic life as distinct from the intellectual and emulative life', aiming to serve in the lower orders of the priesthood.[1] Again he perseveres, but now in disturbing tension with his beloved Sue, who mocks his intellectual archaism and deference and, in all her sexual ambivalence, inspires him to the final form of his ambition: they must be together. Sue leaves her unhappy marriage (to Phillotson) to join her cousin in a 'perfect union' of freely associated companions. His priestly vocation thus definitively annulled, Jude burns his theology books and seeks fulfilment in a reasoned ethical choice beyond the trammels of law and custom.

Jude's ambition has all along been one of transcendence. He yearns to emulate Phillotson, who was, he thinks, 'too clever to bide here any longer – a small sleepy place like [Marygreen]!' (49). He is looking for 'some place which he could call admirable ... a spot in which, without fear of farmers, or hindrance, or ridicule, he could watch and wait, and set himself to some mighty undertaking like the men of old of whom he had heard' (65–6). The carter from whom he has learnt much of what he thinks he knows about Christminster, the 'city of light', confirms the character of the ambition *a contrario* as the negation of ordinary life:

Ah, young man, ... you'd have to get your head screwed on t'other way before you could read what they read there ... O,

---

1   Thomas Hardy, *Jude the Obscure* (1896), ed. and introd. C.H. Sisson, Harmondsworth, 1978, p. 181. Further page references appear in brackets in the main text.

they never look at anything that folks like we can understand ...
On'y foreign tongues used in the days of the Tower of Babel,
when no two families spoke alike. (64)

Yet for Jude the desirable other place is at the same time 'something to anchor on, to cling to', something like the ordinary life
that has been denied to him (65). Christminster is Alma Mater as
well as authority figure, a mother as well as a father. His imagined
convocation of the University's past luminaries – Bolingbroke,
Gibbon, Arnold and Newman, among others – ends in the bathos
of Bishop Ken, the composer of the *Evening Hymn*, a 'meek,
familiar rhyme, endeared to him from earliest childhood' (129).
The other life that he imagines for himself is that of a family.
Culture will redeem him from the loneliness of orphanhood. The
commitment to a life with Sue is a dialectical overcoming of his
early ambition, with its tense opposition between learning and
living (the pattern of his marriage to Arabella Donn), towards a
form of domestic intimacy that is in itself a critique of ordinary
life – and at the same time an imaginary restoration of the ideal
plenitude of infancy.

None of Jude's projects succeeds. The first ends in disappoint-
ment; the second he abandons for the sake of the third, and that
ends in general disaster. What explains these outcomes? The
novel is prolific in suggestion, accommodating incongruous
varieties of explanation and at times courting simple self-contradiction. *Jude* is complex in its discursive constitution. A certain
radicalism of social evaluation presses against a strong current
of naturalistic pessimism that, unsurprisingly, brings with it its
own preferred kinds of justifying conjecture; a passionate Millian

liberalism in the domain of marriage strains against the unshaken sexist commonplaces of the day.[2] The upshot is an ambiguous vision in which all suggestions find some objective narrative support; they may be disputed – as Sue more than once disputes Jude's self-deprecating reflections – but none is falsified. Aunt Drusilla has a staunch belief in the family curse: the Fawleys make bad marriages and a marriage of two Fawleys would be calamitous. Jude is given to blaming a personal weakness for women and drink. Both he and Sue have ready generalizations concerning the natural tendencies of women, and these coexist with general thoughts in a more historical vein, where their misfortunes are attributed to modern 'pushing' and 'restless-ness', impatience and, in less self-punishing moments, social prematurity.

At their most defiant, they hazard more biting terms of evalu-ation. Jude is 'one of the very men Christminster was intended for when the colleges were founded', Sue declares, 'a man with a passion for learning, but no money, or opportunities, or friends'. Yet he has been 'elbowed off the pavement by the millionaires' sons' (205). Jude comes to perceive his situation in similar terms:

> I love the place – although I know how it hates all men like me – the so-called Self-taught, – how it scorns our laboured acquisi-tions, when it should be the first to respect them; how it sneers at our false quantities and mispronunciations, when it should say, I see you want help, my poor friend! (391)

---

2   Resulting in the strange character of Sue, an 'aerial', 'sexless', defiant freethinker. Her contrary, Arabella, all flesh and opportunism, is not strange at all.

This version of things is corroborated by narrative events that do not depend on family superstition or circular commonplaces about character and gender. Jude experiences his first setback early on, when he is dismissed by Farmer Troutham for allowing birds to eat the newly scattered seed, in flat contradiction of his duty, which is to scare them away. The farmer's property, from which Jude is henceforth barred, lies across the path that leads from Marygreen to Christminster. Years later, his innocent reverie of Christminster is cut short by a policeman inquiring 'what you med be up to' (127). In the colleges themselves, his ambitions are promptly dealt with: he is ignored, or advised to 'stick to his trade', repairing the walls that exclude him, just as later he and Sue will maintain the churches by whose writ they will be driven from work and home. Private property, the state and the official culture thus combine against them. 'Something external to us' dictates that they shall not learn, they shall not labour, they shall not love, Sue concludes (412), and that something is a whole social order.

The cause of culture has proved hopeless: Jude's given name is only the first of many ironies suggesting as much. Beyond this, there are various grounds for believing that his cause was not even worthwhile. The impulse is in itself quite clearly infantile. Sue, while supporting Jude in his ambition to learn, is open in her disdain for his specific intellectual commitments and his naive attachment to Christminster, which she derides as 'a place full of fetichists and ghost-seers'. This is a fair description of Jude himself, on his first night in the city, and the narrative generally favours the enlightened, freethinking Sue over her 'obscure' cousin. But there are further displacements at work. Hardy's first published title for his novel was *The Simpletons*, a choice that lays the heaviest emphasis on the lovers as partners in illu-sion.[3] What the illusion might finally consist in is not entirely clear. 'The letter killeth' is the novel's well-known motto, and the balancing clause of the sentence comes easily, even now: 'but the spirit giveth life'.[4] On this interpretation, the crucial stake in the novel is the cousins' free union and its ethical challenge to common opinion (*Hearts Insurgent* was Hardy's next choice of title). But another interpretation would take the motto at its words, seeing the truncated quotation not merely as a recall to the hallowed duty of compassion but as a complete statement with its own reference and meaning. 'The letter killeth': it is the letter itself – literacy, reading, culture – that kills.

Jude seeks what he not only cannot have, but should not even want.[5] Perseverance here must be tragic in sense. Or in other terms, Jude's *Bildung* is an impossibility. Hardy's narrative, as *Bildungsroman*, plots this proposition quite systematically, track-ing not one *Bildung* but four, in a strategy akin to that of the high-naturalist 'experimental novel'.[6] Jude aspires and is frus-trated at every turn; persevering, he loses everything, including his life. Sue likewise perseveres, loses her companion and their children, and ends up morally crushed, one of the 'fetichists and ghost-seers' she used to mock. Phillotson aspires, but not too dangerously: his Christminster vocation is one of a series of temporary enthusiasms, on a par with ancient history and

---

3 For the history of the title of the novel, see 'A Note on the Text', p. 499.

4 2 Corinthians 3:3.

5 The Marygreen constabulary have a point when they conclude that Jude, who has the habit of reading as he drives his horse and cart, is a danger, but mainly to himself (74–5).

6 See Émile Zola, *Le roman expérimental*, Paris, 1880, pp. 1–53.

playing the piano. His one visionary moment is his decision to release Sue from her marriage vows, and for this scandalous act he pays with the loss of his professional status and expectations. But he survives, chastened, to repossess the broken Sue, in the sexual bond he knows she finds repugnant. The plain exception is Arabella, whose rule of life is 'poor folks must live' (111). Alert and resourceful on her own behalf, Arabella never questions the order of priorities and probabilities that society has laid out for people like her, and on those terms she succeeds again and again, surviving to utter the last words of the novel, a prospective requiem for Sue. The comedy of Arabella Donn offers supporting evidence for what the plangent stories of the others already strongly imply: that development and survival are strictly antithetical goals. The letter killeth.

2

Between *Jude the Obscure* (1895–6) and *Howards End* (1910), there is a real lapse of fifteen years, and a fictional interval of a whole generation. That is to say, if both narratives are set in the near-contemporary, as they appear to be, then Jude would have been born around 1865, some twenty-five years before his typological successor, Leonard Bast. Calculations of this kind are simplistic, and must be. Fictional time is elastic and intermittent, however closely familiar chronometry may be simulated. Realist novels in the mass presuppose a common world of some kind, yet, notwithstanding their novel-by-novel verisimilitude, each is finally its own universe. For all that, it remains pertinent to say that as Jude heads towards final defeat, another working-class boy is beginning to be aware of the promise of culture.

One of the fundamental shifts from the earlier novel to the later occurs in the relations between country and city as condensing values. Cities, in *Jude*, are sites of opportunity, for learning and self-fashioning (Jude and Sue) or other new beginnings (Arabella). The village is 'sleepy', confining, sunk in unreflective custom (Jude), and provincial towns are the resting places of small or spent ambitions (Phillotson). In *Howards End*, by contrast, the beckoning city of light has been reimagined as a creeping 'red rust',[7] the deposit of the nineteenth-century 'craze for motion' that may soon overrun Howards End and what it preserves of an older, settled life. The house, which is no longer the home of a farming family but not yet a near-suburban property for rent, marks a historic crux. In it, Forster offers a trope for one of the great themes of English cultural criticism in the twentieth century: 'continuity', the palpable, now threatened moral inheritance of culture. For Margaret and Helen Schlegel, the great anxiety is generated not in the struggle to acquire culture but in the duty to actualize and transmit it.

The appeal to continuity is the temporal axis of Margaret's motto, 'Only connect', and as her own story shows, the corresponding plane of action is synchronic, extending across the prevailing social order of culture. Here too, *Howards End* marks a significant shift from *Jude*. Of course, the commonalities should not be set aside. Leonard Bast is another working-class aspirant to culture; his family bonds, like Jude's, are vestigial, and weakened further by the lineal transposition from country to city; in Jacky he has his own Arabella, another 'unsuitable'

---

7   E.M. Forster, *Howards End* (1910), London, 1941, p. 316. Further page references appear in brackets in the main text.

partner with something of a history; and he will not end well. However, even within the commonalities there is a telling difference to note. Jude's class profile is plain: he is a skilled manual worker. But Bast's social standing seems amenable to disconcerting shifts in perception. Hardy's novel is set in a world of labour with only modest outcroppings of property and learning within its boundaries. Jude may be eccentric and even frictional in this popular world ('Hoity-toity', as Arabella says), but it is his and he remains a protagonist within it, even as the odds mount against him. More pointedly, Jude is indisputably an agent, unlike Bast, whose agency on his own behalf begins to falter the day he meets a lady at a Beethoven recital. Stumbling into the Schlegel purview by a trivial circumstance, he is drawn into a relationship of patronage that will 'help' him to destitution and violent death – another sombre imaginative turn, in a novel written just as an independent party of labour was emerging from Liberal political tutelage and controversy over the strategic priorities of workers' education reached a defining moment with the creation of the Plebs' League at Ruskin College.[8]

Forster's protagonists in the affair are two bourgeois families, the cultured *rentier* Schlegels and the philistine Wilcoxes, who make their money in imperial trade. It is this relationship – one between two class fractions of capital – that lies nearer the heart of Forster's concern and advocacy in *Howards End*. In this too,

---

8   The Labour Representation Committee, created in 1900, won twenty-nine parliamentary seats in the British general election of 1906 and at that point proclaimed 'The Labour Party'; the Plebs' League was founded in 1908 in the struggle for an independent alternative to the educational conceptions in official favour at Ruskin College, a centre for working-class learning itself not yet ten years old (f. 1899).

there is an important difference from *Jude*, which is radical in that it sees and engages the established culture from the places of the 'obscure'. Forster, in contrast, inscribes his novel within the received terms of English discourse on culture, in an explicit revision of the Arnoldian tradition.

Howards End belongs to that broad class of narratives dramatizing the conflict between the bohemian and the bourgeois. The Schlegels devote themselves to the arts and schemes of social reform; by virtue of early inheritance, the sisters are both leisured and autonomous, living as they please. The Wilcox family, in contrast, is organized for business, good sense and the maintenance of order in general. The Schlegels, of German and English parentage, are cosmopolitan, or easily taken to be so, and certainly not 'British', which the Wilcoxes decidedly are, not least because the Empire is their sphere of operations. Falling into company with them on a holiday in Germany, the sisters take note of Wilcox ways, and set their expectations accordingly; and the conflict that follows upon Helen's rebellion and the final revelation of her pregnancy conforms to stock expectations on both sides. By that time, however, the basic terms of the Schlegel-Wilcox opposition have been complicated, ironized and even subverted by the movement of Forster's narrative.

The first intimation of this comes very early, in a domain where the opposition seems set firm: that of gender. Wickham Place, the Schlegel family home, 'is a female house', Margaret affirms, and always has been, even in their father's day: 'It must be feminine', in contrast with the Wilcox's house, which sounds to her 'irrevocably masculine', so that 'all its inmates can do is to see that it isn't brutal' (43). Necessarily feminine – but she has added: 'and all we can do is to see that it isn't effeminate'. The balance of her judgement is at least as important as its trenchancy, and not at all hypothetical. Helen has anticipated it, both generally and in plain particulars, in her first letter to Margaret from the Wilcox family home at Howards End, where she has accepted an invitation to visit. 'It isn't going to be what we expected', she begins, referring to the house, '… it isn't the least what we expected'. Then, complaining of their younger brother's mannered hypochondria (which has kept Margaret at home), she writes: 'Tell him that Charles Wilcox … has hay fever too, but he's brave and gets cross when we inquire after it. Men like the Wilcoxes would do Tibby the power of good' (5). 'You won't agree', Helen adds, but Margaret will come to agree, and also to reflect progressively on the financial conditions of her independence, on the class-privileges she shares with the Wilcoxes, and on what society in general and Schlegels in particular may owe to them: 'Last night [she says to her aunt], I began to think that the very soul of the world is economic, and that the lowest abyss is not the absence of love, but the absence of coin' (58). And later, to Helen: 'More and more do I refuse to draw my income and sneer at those who guarantee it' (164). Margaret's newly reflexive apprehension of her class situation, which develops in step with her affection for Henry Wilcox, now cohabits with an older interest in those she habitually calls 'the poor', who have recently taken proximate shape in the person of Leonard Bast. Bast is one of the novel's more complex figural elements. He is an office clerk – that is, a worker, in a word that occurs nowhere in *Howards End*. His poverty is emphasized and detailed; if not actually 'in the abyss, … he could see it, and at times people whom he knew had dropped in …' (44).[9] Cockney, he is also said 'to stand at the extreme verge of gentility', to be 'one of those who are obliged to pretend that they are gentlefolk' (44). Margaret, at their first meeting, reflects that 'his class was near enough her own for its manners to vex her' – a curious thought for a leisured lady to have about a penniless clerk (36). Bast is incongruously formed, because of the kind of being he stands for: he is not a representative of an inherited or achieved status and function, like the Schlegels and Wilcoxes or the assorted porters and domestics who move in the margins of the narrative, but a blurred snapshot of historical movement, a tendency or a portent, a worker sapped by estrangement from his rural antecedents and now hungry for more than his present smattering of Culture. Bast is out of place, a taxonomic oddity, and in that sense monstrous. His presence has a power of disturbance well in excess of any individual capability the novel grants him. The Schlegels have devoted themselves to 'the unseen', with an uncertain, though hardly diffident, sense of what philanthropic obligations that might entail. Now, into the 'politico-economical-aesthetic atmosphere' of Wickham Place, comes an unexpected 'goblin footfall'.[10]

It is, the sentence continues, 'a hint that all is not for the best in the best of all possible worlds, and that beneath these

---

9 The metaphor of the abyss, so emphatic throughout *Howards End*, was still fresh from Jack London's first-hand account of the English capital's East End, *The People of the Abyss* (1903) – a book in which *Jude the Obscure* was already a byword for working-class intellectual aspiration. (London's real-world case was a dockers leader, Dan Cullen.)

10 Or two: Jacky is a second goblin footfall: she has in fact 'risen out of the abyss, like a faint smell' and her appearance is 'awesome' (108, 49). 'The Unseen' is another of Jack London's phrases.

superstructures of wealth and art there wanders an ill-fed boy, who has recovered his umbrella indeed, but who has left no address behind him, and no name' (44). Bast is hungry, transient and obscure. All he can show is his umbrella, the index of his desire and his confusion, his elision of culture and gentility. The judgement implicit in that serio-comic item (as in the characteristic narratorial facetiousness that plays around its owner) is prompt and also final. Bast's fate is intimated before he is even named. The last clause of the sentence, in a sly prolepsis, gathers the particulars of an awkward afternoon's encounter into a summing up of a whole life.

Nothing in the novel suggests that Bast may be the equal of his cultural aspirations. Jacky has no understanding of the desires that move him. The Schlegels are openly impatient of his deference towards 'beautiful books' – 'a swamp of books', in truth, which he mistakes for ends rather than the 'sign-posts' they merely are. He himself is easily discouraged. Yet Margaret and Helen are persuaded that he has 'spirit', and resolve to help him, with disastrous results. Having been advised, on mistaken grounds, to leave a secure job, then lost another one that appeared more dependable but was not, Bast fears he is unemployable. A second, melodramatic intervention by the 'absolutist' Helen, who longs 'to have raised one person from the abyss' (237), leaves him and Jacky homeless and reduced to beggary, and Helen pregnant – a circumstance that will lead to his death at the hand of an angry younger Wilcox, Charles, and burial under the contents of the Schlegel bookcase he clings to as he falls.

Throughout, these dramas are encoded in the terms of Matthew Arnold's tribute to Sophocles, the exemplary ancient 'who saw life steadily, and saw it whole'.[11] The changeable relationship between the two predicative terms – the ideal possibility of their combination and the implications of a disjunctive turn – enacts the moral crisis of the novel *in nuce*.

'Steadily' is, first of all, how the drum beats in a certain passage of Beethoven's Fifth Symphony, according to Tibby, who shares nothing of Helen's impulse to turn musical experience into literature and, therefore, moral incident (37). It is how Bast imagines women must read from childhood 'to acquire culture' (39), and how he himself reads in his attempt to learn his style from Ruskin, whom he takes for 'the greatest master of English Prose' (48). All three illustrations are marked as poor – reductive because purely technical or sadly naive. When steadiness rejoins its ideal partner it is again in Bast's estimate of what is possible – or rather, not possible. Culture is beyond the reach of those not born to it, he fears: 'To see life steadily and to see it whole was not for the likes of him' (53).

But neither is it for those who have been born to it, Margaret comes to believe. She perceives, from her privileged vantage-point, what Bast fears, looking up from below. When Arnold's words make their first appearance in her reflections – more than two years later – it is with a significant revision, in a disjunctive form that calls for reparative measures. 'It is impossible to see modern life steadily and see it whole, and she had chosen to see it whole.' Mr Wilcox, on the other hand,

---

11   In full it reads: 'But be his / My special thanks, whose even-balanced soul, / From first youth tested up to extreme old age, / Business could not make dull, nor passion wild; / Who saw life steadily, and saw it whole…' (Arnold, 'To a Friend', 1848–1849).

> saw steadily. He never bothered over the mysterious or the
> private. ... Yet she liked being with him. ... Some day – in the
> millennium – there may be no need for his type. At present,
> homage is due to it from those who think themselves superior,
> and who possibly are. (152)

In Tibby, the risk of decadence is already manifest, and it may
be that the Schlegel sisters' proud grasp of the whole is slacken-
ing into sociable indiscrimination: 'She found him interesting on
the whole': this is Margaret, freely reported within minutes of
making Bast's acquaintance. 'Everyone interested the Schlegels
on the whole at that time – and while her lips talked culture, her
heart was planning to invite him to tea' (36–7).

Soon, Margaret will accept Henry as 'her lord', and 'steady'
will describe the manner of their growing affection for each
other (162, 242). But Margaret's conversion is to irony, not
an alternative absolute. She does not cease to note 'the breezy
Wilcox manner', which lacks 'the clearness of vision that is
imperative for truth' (170). Businessmen see 'more steadily',
the narrator will later comment, 'though with the steadiness of
the half-closed eye' (301). In this comedy of modern manners,
the warrant of an undivided life resides in the figure who never
let go of the past and has now become a part of it: Henry's late
wife, Ruth, the mistress of Howards End. She has been singled
out from the first, by Helen, for her 'steady unselfishness' – not
quite canonical Arnold, but a compelling maternal avatar of
Arnoldian disinterestedness. She belongs to Howards End and
to what it can give of the 'feeling of completeness': 'In these
English farms, if anywhere, one might see life steadily and see
it whole, group in one vision its transitoriness and its eternal

youth, connect — connect without bitterness until all men are brothers' (250).

In *Howards End*, Forster put to his own liberal culture the question of its constitutive social dependencies: most clearly its dependence on an illiberal entrepreneurial class fraction that it conventionally disdained, but also, though less clearly, its dependence on a labouring population to which it extended little more than disquieted solicitude. In that gesture lies the critical distinction of the novel: the risk it ran and the exceptional rhetorical challenge it thereby set itself. In short: after such knowledge, what resolution? The whole array of comic invention, from censorship — in the figural forms of mockery, exile and death — to transfiguration, is deployed to manage the effects of that critical question: not quite to withdraw it but to stage it in answerable forms.

The narrative process is forthright. Tibby is spotlit from the beginning: the languid, self-absorbed excess of leisure-class cultivation, he must be displaced to the margins, as must his Wilcox counterpart, Charles, who has perfected the bullying, brutal tendencies of the muscular bourgeoisie. Indeed, Tibby is twice polarized, first as a parasitic variety of the bourgeois but then also as the opposite of the proletarian Jacky Bast. He is the over-rarefied creature of culture, she the obese and stupid epitome of not-culture, and together (within a few pages) they will disappear from the narrative, each having been briefly roused from sleep by Leonard Bast, who is making his way to Howards End, increasingly tormented by feelings of remorse for his sexual encounter with Helen. Charles too is twice polarized, and his typological negative, again in general class terms and also culturally, is

Leonard: what the clerk yearns for, the businessman fears as so much 'artistic beastliness'. Bast will die and Charles, convicted of his manslaughter, will go to prison and then into social exile. There remain, then, Margaret and the principal rivals for her attention, Henry and Helen, and the unsettled fate of Howards End. Her husband and sister cannot be simply dispatched or simply reconciled. Their contrariety is formative and abiding; the very idea of the novel presupposes it. However, they can be chastened and moderated. Both have wronged the Basts, and both are tempered by the ulterior consequences of their actions: Henry is 'broken' by scandal – not the story of his old adulterous affair with Jacky, which remains suppressed, but Charles's – and Helen is subdued by irregular motherhood. In these conditions, equalized as 'invalids', they can at least 'connect'.

Margaret undergoes a change of another kind. As the novel opens, it is disconnection that sets the mood. This is at once general and historic – it is the civilization of 'luggage' – and particular: the Schlegels are soon to lose their family home in Wickham Place and Henry Wilcox is impatient for an alternative to his wife's family home. These are the circumstances in which Margaret and Ruth become friends. What Ruth is has already been established in authoritative and telling terms:

> One knew that she worshipped the past, and that the instinctive wisdom the past can alone bestow had descended upon her – that wisdom to which we give the clumsy name of aristocracy. High born she might not be. But assuredly she cared about her ancestors, and let them help her. (22)

Here is the paramount value of the novel, and, in discovering her affinity with Ruth, Margaret accedes to it as a moral space beyond the conventional bourgeois antagonism mostly starkly represented by the young men of their households. She has been marked out as morally privileged from the beginning, the only character to be associated with the 'wisdom' of the impersonal narrative voice, even giving the novel its motto, 'Only connect'. The transfiguring movement of the narrative is her assimilation to the status of the second Mrs Wilcox, chosen by Henry but also, and earlier, by Ruth, as her 'spiritual heir', the new mistress of Howards End.

Edged with satire in its critical movement, the narrative is deeply romantic in its contrapuntal upward curve, at times approaching the marvellous. Aunt Juley, who embodies all that is unsympathetic about the dominant Englishness – jingoism, xenophobia and bossy good form – dies and is succeeded in the role of helper by Miss Avery, an elderly neighbour at Howards End. It is she who spontaneously works the wonder of reconstructing the Wickham Place interior in the old farmhouse and who immediately discerns the true line of inheritance, mistaking Margaret at first sighting for the dead Ruth Wilcox herself. She is the avatar of another England, one already glimpsed in passages of transfigured landscape,[12] and now localized in the hayfield at Howards End, a pastoral setting in which Margaret looks after Henry and Helen and the unnamed child through whom Bast will be restored to an English farm where, 'if anywhere', he may see life steadily and see it whole.

---

12   See the opening paragraphs of Chapter 19.

This radiant finale is in the high tradition of social comedy, but the complex feeling of the last sequence as a whole is the reminder that it is only a moment. The multi-modal quality of *Howards End*, with its attendant displacements of tone, may be read as an index of agitation, of the anxious labour of writing by which the stark questions of the novel are negotiated towards the resolution-effect of the finale. Just how much effect and how little resolution there is in that finale, for all its summer light and exultation, can be seen more clearly when we formalize the narrative semantics of the novel, so in effect mapping its historical imagination. The semiotic square (Figure 1) sets out the basic coordinates of the fictional situation, which are set by the contrariety between the *cultured* and the *philistine* as bourgeois dispositions.[13] Each implies its necessary opposite, the *uncultured*

---

13   The semiotic square, a logico-rhetorical device of Aristotelian provenance, now mainly associated with the structural semantics of A. J. Greimas and given wider currency in Fredric Jameson's creative use of it, is a means of formalizing the semantics of any verbal communication. (See Algirdas Julien Greimas, *On Meaning*, with a foreword by Fredric Jameson, Minneapolis, 1987.) Simply and briefly, any text is structured by a contrariety, a non-necessary opposition that defines the upper horizontal of the square. These contrary terms logically generate their negations, termed contradictories, which then form a second set of contraries (the lower horizontal). The contraries, as contingent oppositions, are in principle resolvable, unlike the contradictories (the diagonal oppositions) which are opposites by definition and therefore not resolvable. The vertices at the top and bottom, left and right of the figure, indicate the available or suggested resolutions. In other, more concrete terms, the semiotic square maps the semantic poles of any given narrative, its necessities and the implicit rules governing what is possible and what is not possible in the given instance – or what in another tradition of thought might be called its imagination. The vertices indicate the possible narrative outcomes. In not a few cases, this formalizing procedure adds little to what is anyway evident, but in others it can be a powerful interpretive

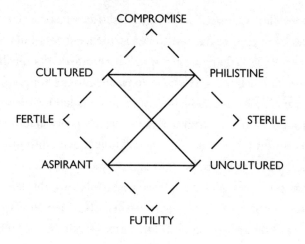

Figure 1 *Howards End*

and the *aspirant*, which then make a second contingent opposition, the sub-contraries. The contradictories are the impossible terms of resolution, and the action of the novel confirms what the scheme indicates: Tibby and Jacky never actually come face to face, and when Charles and Leonard meet, the consequences are disastrous for both of them. Among the contraries and their possible resolutions, the liaison between the philistine bourgeois and the uncultured proletarian is sterile (Henry and Jacky), and that between two working-class types, the aspirant and the uncultured (the Basts), proves futile. The intra-class rapprochement of cultured and philistine is impossible at the extremes (Tibby and

---

tool, offering unexpected insights. However, it not an easy one to use: much depends on the accuracy of the interpreter's first intuitions, and if any of the basic oppositions is misidentified to start with, the operation will be frustrated. More fundamentally, the logic of the square seems to presuppose coherence in the texts it maps – a dogmatic general assumption guaranteed to produce its own set of hard cases.

Charles) but manageable nevertheless (Margaret and Henry),
though with the proviso that the imago of reconciliation is a dead
mother, Ruth Wilcox, whose spiritual successor has resolved to
remain childless, so setting a term to a future of bourgeois self-
sufficiency. The new heir to Howards End has different parents:
the fourth vertex, by contrast, is fertile. The encounter between
the cultured bourgeois and the working-class aspirant (Helen
and Leonard) produces a child and thus a future – but on clear,
hard terms. Bast himself is dead, weakened by the hereditary
physical decline of his class and finished off by the consequences
of his aspiration to culture. ('The letter killeth' again.) The son
to whom the future belongs will be a second-generation leisure-
class intellectual, born to culture as his father was not. His mother
admits that she is already forgetting the father and is urged (by
Margaret) to let it be so. The price of Bast's symbolic victory,
if it is even that, is the extinction of himself and his memory.
One kind of reading will emphasize the ambiguity of this, and
find in *Howards End* a lesson in historical realism: there can be
no universal access to culture in a class society and the attempt
to anticipate a more equal state of things is deforming, attain-
ing nothing better than a genteel simulation, and destined to fail.
Another reading will see in it the Arnoldian vision of 'English
civilization': 'the humanizing, the bringing into one harmonious
and truly humane life, of the whole body of English society' –
or the assimilation of independent working-class aspiration to a
rejuvenated liberal-bourgeois ecumene.[14]

---

14   Matthew Arnold, 'Ecce, Convertimur ad Gentes' (a lecture given at
the Working Men's College, Ipswich), *Irish Essays and Others*, London, 1882,
p. 118.

2. *The Aristocratic Fix*

At the heart of the matter of culture is the house. All the great general issues in play in *Howards End* can be rendered within the scope of this topos. It is in the nature of the house, or the presumptive entitlement to it, to be at risk, as part of a wider crisis of continuity. All that is implicit in the right of inheritance, which is also a duty to succeed, is under threat. Pressing enough in the bourgeois world of *Howards End*, such issues are inescapably central in the social zone to which the condition of culture novel withdrew in the decades after the First World War, in the hands of Virginia Woolf and Evelyn Waugh, now taking as its touchstone of cultural value the great houses of aristocracy such as Brideshead and Orlando's vast ancestral seat.

This withdrawal is the leading aspect of a displacement in social-historical time, whose concomitant is recoil from the sites and stakes of modern class relations – the ground on which Hardy and Forster had advanced their reflections on the condition of culture. Woolf, in *Orlando*, gaily suspends the ordinary fatalities of sexed, mortal being and, with them, the disturbing presence of the middle classes – to say nothing of the labouring population beyond and below them, who appear only as household retainers, not the sort who not long ago might have made revolutions in Russia and Germany or even, much closer to the English here and now, a general strike. Waugh, not enjoying Woolf's great licence and writing at a further temporal remove, acknowledges the strike of 1926 but at the distance of rumour and legend, as an interlude in a life whose keynote, not yet silenced, is aristocracy.

I

One day during the summer of his 'aesthetic education' at Brideshead, Charles Ryder asks his friend Sebastian Flyte how the family home, a splendid Palladian mansion, came to be called 'Castle':

'It used to be one until they moved it.'

'What can you mean?'

'Just that. We had a castle a mile away, down by the village. Then we took a fancy to the valley and pulled the castle down, carted the stones up here, and built a new house. I'm glad they did, aren't you?'[1]

This is a rich exchange, notable for its swift epitome of propertied caprice (and corresponding occlusion of those who actually did the pulling down and carting and building), which is confirmed

---

1   Evelyn Waugh, *Brideshead Revisited: The Sacred and Profane Memories of Captain Charles Ryder* (1945), London, 2000, p. 77. Further page references appear in brackets in the main text.

now in the simple narcissism of Sebastian's account ('I'm glad …
aren't you?'). It is notable also for its pronoun switches, in which
Waugh captures the ontological specificity of the property and
power that Brideshead represents. Sebastian's easy movement
from *they* to *we* and back again expresses the basic principle of an
aristocracy of blood: the inherence of lineage in biography.

For Sebastian himself, the principle is a mortmain that will
be the end of him. For an earlier fictional representative of his
kind, it is a life-force beyond ordinary nature. In Woolf's character Orlando, the ontology implied in Sebastian's pronominal
usage finds its most remarkable avatar. Living for more than
three hundred years, from the late sixteenth century, and ageing
no more than twenty years in that time, with uncounted years
still to come, Orlando is not merely a character whose attributes
include blue blood: the marvellous temporal duality that defines
his being is nobility itself, the line as the eternalizing quality of
the life, or the life as the abiding presence of the lineage. What is
more, this is not Orlando's only marvellous attribute. He is also
capable of spontaneous trans-sexual metamorphosis, becoming a woman, without warning and, it seems, permanently, at
the age of thirty and remaining so for the next six (that is, two
hundred plus) years of her life. *Orlando* is most often remembered today for its critical reflection on an oppressive culture of
gender and sexuality and its fabulation of a depolarized, mobile
subjectivity beyond it. To strike a different emphasis now is not
to diminish the significance of this central concern, but – inevitably – to show it in another light. Woolf's notion of androgyny,
of the necessary coexistence of the woman-manly and the man-
womanly and their changeable balance in subjective life, includes
a norm of wholeness against which sex as such is, as she says,

a 'distraction': transgression in the plane of sexuality is from time to time drawn a step beyond, to a state more closely akin to transcendence, and in this it converges with the wholeness that belongs to the idealizing self-image of aristocracy, for which the unity of the *vita activa* and the *vita contemplativa* in the Renaissance man is the historically pertinent reference.[2] Orlando, as courtier, diplomat, poet and lover, is already a paragon of the type, but then excels himself in outliving the age and escaping the half-life of existence as a mere man in a world of two sexes. The Lady Orlando, a Renaissance man become modern woman, sets a new standard of perfection.

The perfection is aristocratic nonetheless, as also is the significance of another marvel in Orlando's life, her pregnancy. How does this come about? There is no identifiable father, in realist terms. It is not excluded that she has been made pregnant as it were allegorically, by the Victorian *Zeitgeist*, with its essentialist cult of motherhood. But it is also possible – and in keeping with much else in the novel – that the begetter of her son is her own male self. The trans-sexual metamorphosis is then the means by which Orlando relays the line of his 'fathers' (Woolf's recurring synecdoche) into an 'infinitely noble' – because male – future.[3] (Only the sons can inherit.) In a startling reversal of the feminist utopian tradition, Orlando not only figures the perdurance of blue blood itself but also realizes its androcentric fantasy of parthenogenesis for men.[4] Whereas Helen Schlegel's pregnancy

2 See *Culture/Metaculture* (London, 2000) for a discussion of Woolf's *A Room of One's Own*.

3 Virginia Woolf, *Orlando: A Biography* (1928), Harmondsworth, 1942, p. 9. Further page references appear in brackets in the main text.

4 Charlotte Perkins Gilman's *Herland* (1915) imagined a remote society

is the outcome of a tense, star-crossed encounter between a bourgeois and a worker, with their discrepant visions of the future,
Orlando's announces aristocratic self-sufficiency without end,
in a fantastical negation of the cultural order that was Forster's
critical fictional object.

Nobility and androgyny are two decisive modalities of
Orlando's being; the third is literature. He has read and written
devotedly since boyhood and is a compulsive minter of rhymes
and conceits. The literary spirit of the age works in him, so that
he is hyperbolic among Tudors and melancholy in the time of Sir
Thomas Browne – and so on into the twentieth century, when her
subjectivity takes a cubo-futurist turn. The value of what (s)he
writes will be tested repeatedly, by the standards of 'Literature'
and those of 'Life' – a distinction at once basic and ill-founded in
the novel, where nothing is less certain than that the two categories are not in some way one.

Orlando, hoping for confirmation that 'he himself belonged
to the sacred race rather than the noble – [that he] was by birth
a writer, rather than an aristocrat' (49) – solicits a visit from the
famous writer Nicholas Greene, for the benefit of his insight and
judgement. The results are disturbing. The judgement, when it
comes, takes the form of public mockery, and the insight is economic: poetry is 'harder to sell than prose' and takes longer to
write (51). Furthermore, Greene's presence – boastful, mali-
cious, calculating – is itself upsetting:

> Orlando, for all his knowledge of mankind, was puzzled where
> to place him. There was something about him which belonged

---

of women rendered sexually self-sufficient by the spontaneous development
of a parthenogenetic faculty.

neither to servant, squire or noble. ... There was nothing of that
stately composure which makes the faces of the nobility so pleas-
ing to look at; nor had it anything of the dignified servility of a
well-trained domestic's face. (50)

He comes to fear, as he reflects on this first acquaintance with
a bourgeois man of letters, that he has 'admitted to his house
a plaguey spirit of unrest that would never suffer him to sleep
sound again'.[5]

Orlando now renounces the public institution of Literature,
with its crowning value of Fame – or 'Glawr' (*gloire*), as Greene
has it – and gives himself to the 'dark, ample' freedom of 'obscurity' (61). Obscurity, as he now perceives it, is an ethic, which
has its monument in the great, unnamed mansion he has inherited and its exemplary instance in the historic life-process of the
household.

Here have lived, for more centuries than I can count, the obscure
generations of my own obscure family [including, as the natural
complement of the noble line, the servants]. Not one of these
Richards, Johns, Annes, Elizabeths has left a token of himself
behind him, yet all, working together with their spades and their
needles, their love-making and their child-bearing have left this.
... Lords though [his kinsmen] were, they were content to go
down into obscurity with the mole-catcher and the stonemason.
(62–3)

---

5   Nick Greene's real-world near-contemporary and counterpart,
Robert Greene (1558–1592), was one of the first literary professionals in
London, living by his pen and reputedly managing even his personal notori-
ety for pecuniary advantage. See also note 6 following.

Of ethical and also aesthetic significance, the house is the product of an 'anonymous work of creation' that none should presume to better, and in this sense the care of the house is not an alternative to poetry but an equivalent. Orlando brings his eloquence to the life of the household and as he does so, coordinates and condenses the two: 'Whatever [his] peroration wanted, that was what the house stood in need of. Leaving his speech unfinished for the moment, he ... resolved henceforward to devote himself to the furnishing of the mansion' (63). Equivalent and perhaps superior, in truth, for obscurity 'must have been the way of all great poets', he muses, of church-builders and of Shakespeare – who just may have been the unnamed writer Orlando once chanced to see in the servants' quarters and has never since ceased wondering about. The house as Orlando knows it is haunted by Shakespeare, and the tangible counterpart of that spiritual presence is a solitary oak, high on a hill in the park, a point of vantage like Forster's Purbeck Hills, offering a synoptic vision of the great house and all England. Uniting the house and the country as microcosm to macrocosm, the oak tree also provides the title of Orlando's earliest and last remaining literary undertaking, the poem he goes on writing over centuries.

Fame comes anyway. *The Oak Tree* is published with the assistance of a canny Victorian Nicholas Greene and becomes a commercial and critical success. But the novel's spiral integration of literature and life has already taken a further turn. Writing poetry is properly thought of as 'a secret transaction', Orlando now believes, 'a voice answering a voice. ... What could have been more secret, she thought, more slow, and like the intercourse of lovers' than the unfinished poem she has kept at her breast all these centuries? (187) More like – say – her relationship with Marmaduke Bonthrop Shelmerdine, whom she has married within days of their dramatic midnight encounter on the moor. Here, perhaps, is the culminating 'ecstasy' of 'life'. But even now the spiral continues, for Shel, a ship's captain whose vocation is braving the seas around Cape Horn, is himself literature – an adventure story for boys – and Orlando the poet has been literature all along, a literary descendant of the warrior Roland, bearing the name of one of the great heroes of Renaissance literature.[6] The wild goose that starts from cover in the closing scene of the novel, prompting her final, fragmentary utterance, is perhaps intended as a trope of life beyond the reach of literature, and might even be read as such, were it not already collocated with the almost ineffable 'Sh – p – re' (180, 189). The image of Shakespeare joins that of Orland's first great love – 'a girl in Russian trousers', from the days of the Frost Fair in 1607 – and her new 'rash', 'ridiculous' seafaring husband in an overwhelming climax: ' "Ecstasy!" she cried, "ecstasy!" And then the wind sank, the waters grew calm; and she saw the waves rippling peacefully in the moonlight' (188). Here is the apotheosis of androgyny, a vision of sexual wholeness now intimately allied with the wholeness and peace of exemplary art.[7] The passage is unmistakably erotic – autoerotic, for Orlando is alone here, as (s)he has been at critical junctures in the novel. ('"I am alone",

---

6   Ludovico Ariosto's *Orlando furioso* (1516–1532) was translated into English by royal command in 1591. The following year saw the performance of a dramatic adaptation of the work, *The History of Orlando Furioso*, written, as it happened, by Robert Greene.

7   The association between Shakespeare and the calm of moonlight is regular in *Orlando*. Shakespeare was for Woolf what Sophocles was for Arnold and his posterity. See *A Room of One's Own* and my discussion in *Culture/Metaculture*, pp. 28–35.

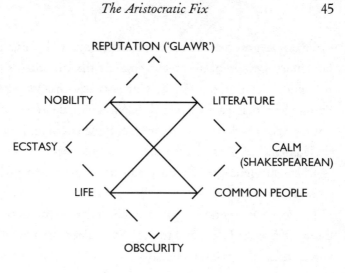

Figure 2 *Orlando*

he breathed at last, opening his lips for the first time…' [11].)
It points to the deepest peculiarity of the work, which semantic
formalization helps to illuminate (Figure 2).

Orlando is first of all *noble*, and it is as such that he submits
to the test of the even more exalted value of the sacred, that is,
literature, in the person of Greene. These are the main contraries
of the narrative, and their respective contradictories are *life* and
the common people, the first represented above all by the Turkish
gypsies with whom she travels after the metamorphosis (but also
by the Russian Sasha, who resists poetic elaboration), the second
by Orlando's servants and casual sexual partners. What narrative outcomes can be plotted from these givens? The resolution
of the main contrariety would be *reputation* – Greene's 'Glawr'
– which Orlando achieves with the publication of *The Oak Tree*.
Its symmetrical opposite – the resolution of the secondary contrariety – is *obscurity*, an alternative mode of creativity to which

Orlando devotes himself for a whole passage in his life as the hereditary steward of his great house. To the left of the square, resolution lies in the *ecstatic* union between Orlando and her daring sea captain; and its specular opposite on the right, resolving the relations between literature and the common people, is the supreme *calm* of Shakespeare – or, perhaps, Orlando, for (s)he has an admixture of common blood, from a milkmaid in the ancestral line.

In short, there is no narrative outcome that excludes or even disadvantages Orlando, and this is possible because none of the narrative givens excludes him. He is, from the outset, noble and (just a little) common, poetic and sexually active. His only limitation – 'for there could be no doubt about his sex' (9) – undoes itself in good time, creating an unchallengeable ideal of cultural wholeness, to which even the bourgeois Greene renders service in the end. Of course Shakespeare remains peerless – even if he, of necessity, has written only the works of Shakespeare, while Orlando, after more than three hundred years of devotion to *The Oak Tree*, has written English literature.[8]

The ideal Woolf explored in the figure of Orlando is, then, not only aristocratic but deeply narcissistic. Everything in the novel is in some sense or another subordinate to, a function of, Orlando's development, which is not the outcome of transforming contact with others – as in Margaret's case in *Howards End*, for example – but rather a process of self-elaboration, the unfolding of what is inborn. *Orlando* is a narrative of classification in which there is only one significant class. Elsewhere, in a

---

8   See Ruth Gruber's remarkable early study, *Virginia Woolf: The Will to Create as a Woman* (1935), New York, 2005.

companion essay, Woolf granted substantial independent reality to the social others of her ideal 'highbrow': the 'lowbrows', with whom they had strong affinities, and the 'middlebrow', the bugbear of both.[9] In this novel, the case is simpler. The servants are organic modalities of their master/mistress; the one and only bourgeois, Greene, fakes noble antecedents and devotes himself to the accumulation of honorific titles; no other cultural horizon is discernible. Nothing is permitted to inhibit the euphoric affirmation of culture as aristocracy.

2

The prevailing manner of *Orlando* is light and whimsical. *Between the Acts*, in contrast, opens on a note of scabrous incongruity and quickly establishes an imagery of natural violence that will persist as the novel's interpretive ground-bass. 'What a subject to talk about on a night like this!' says one of the characters – the company has been discussing a cesspool – but the night, as is soon made known to readers, is in the summer of 1939.[10] The action of the novel, which was published just two years later, is overhung by a political crisis that will very soon explode in a new world war – of which, however, there will be no mention and very little thought. The violence that haunts the narrative is that of blindly appetitive nature, but it is also historical: 'From an aeroplane, [Mr Oliver] said, you could still see the scars made by the Britons; by the Romans; by the Elizabethan manor house; and

9   See 'Middlebrow' in Virginia Woolf, *The Death of the Moth and Other Essays*, London, 1942.

10   Virginia Woolf, *Between the Acts* (1941), New York, 1970, p. 3. Further page references appear in brackets in the main text.

by the plough, when they ploughed the hill to grow wheat in the Napoleonic wars' (4). The extent of the wounds is epochal, civilizational – and the next day, as it happens, will see the enactment in Mr Oliver's grounds of a village pageant depicting the course of English civilization from Elizabeth to the present. Written by one woman, a Miss La Trobe, and performed by the people of the village, this work repeats the chronological traverse of Orlando's long poem, *The Oak Tree*, and of *Orlando* itself, but in a context that shifts all the coordinates of the novel, negating its cultural evaluation.

Pointz Hall, where the action of the novel unfolds, is a house perhaps five hundred years old, 'in the very heart of England', and indeed its grounds are the direct inspiration for the pageant. It is modest enough, nevertheless, and its owners are equally so. Not connected with 'the old families' of the area, they have lived at the Hall for just over a century, and hold their title to it by the fact of purchase, not inheritance. The Olivers are country-dwelling bourgeoisie. Old Bartholomew is a retired colonial administrator; his son, Giles, who had wanted to farm, is unhappily settled in London stock-broking. The manifest record of lineage is sparse (a fact that goes some way to explain his sister Mrs Swithin's fanciful interest in the palaeontology of southern England), and the grounds for social precedence in Giles's wife Isa's family are either adventitious (her father's knighthood) or fanciful (her aunts' descent from the kings of Ireland). The servants themselves, in contrast, are snobs of their kind, bearers of old local names who do their work with due respect for their employers, but nothing like devotion.

Bourgeois and ill-rooted by the prevailing standard, the Olivers are a cultural miscellany. Mrs Swithin combines her taste for Wellsian natural history with a belief in divine providence – which her freethinking brother cruelly mocks. Isa spends much of her waking time amidst half-remembered lines of poetry and is herself a poet, though feeling she must conceal the evidence from her husband, who for his part has no gift for metaphor but can hum *Pop Goes the Weasel*. Pointz Hall's library suggests the overall pattern of the family culture. The higher aspiration embodied in it appears only as risible cliché: the library is 'the heart of the house', and its books are 'the mirrors of the soul'. These have always been an assortment, and they grow now only in the way that debris grows: the later additions are 'shilling shockers' bought by weekend visitors to ease the tedium of the rail journey from London, then 'dropped'.

The house-party on the afternoon of the pageant consists of the four adult Olivers and two unexpected lunch-guests, the wealthy, vulgar, faintly disreputable Mrs Manresa and her protégé William Dodge, who is introduced as an artist. Eros is the unspoken dominant in their social intercourse and, in this too, the novel sets a pattern starkly contrasting with *Orlando*. Orlando is never entirely without sexual ambiguity, even in his rakish cherry-picking heyday at the end of the sixteenth century; and just over one hundred years later, she has entered into the fullness of her trans-sexual androgyny. *Between the Acts*, in contrast, is centred on the drama of a conventionally married couple. Isa knows that 'she never looked like Sappho, or one of the beautiful young men whose photographs adorned the weekly papers' (16). Giles is homophobic: quickly deciding that Dodge is gay, he directs all his unspoken anger towards him. The Olivers are in crisis. Giles is unfaithful, and now Isa is falling in love with a neighbour, whom she hopes in vain to see at the pageant. Mrs Manresa, meanwhile, is pursuing Giles, with some chance of success. If Isa is Mrs Manresa's rival, her opposite is Miss La Trobe, the creator of the pageant, an artist to Manresa's noisy philistine and a settled lesbian. Patterned in this way, the sexuality of this small society implies a bleak estimate of cultural possibility: an ill-considered union of sensibility and money is failing; the two representatives of art, being homosexuals of different sexes, are typologically improbable as a couple, while the heterosexual liaison now in prospect is a meeting of like-minded barbarians, 'the wild child' Manresa and her 'fierce, untamed' Giles. In them, culture succumbs to sociability, which is itself regressing to the condition of bare nature.

The failure of sociability – of 'the common effort' towards 'common meaning', of 'any common conclusion' (152, 186) – is equally damaging, as the experience of the pageant makes plain. La Trobe is aligned with Dodge, as aesthete and homosexual, but opposed to him in her relationship to the action of the novel. He is marginal, the guest of an uninvited guest, and confirms his marginality by his self-effacing manner. She, contrastingly, is self-assertive, like Manresa, though not at all exhibitionist. She is a public figure, both by personal habit and by civic commitment – 'Bossy' is her nickname in the village pub, where she is a regular – and on this day she is central, as the maker of the pageant. The event is chaotic. For some, including Mrs Swithin, it is a moment of personal fulfilment; others are affronted by its want of patriotic decorum, or startled by its more radical tactics of presentation; and there is widespread anxiety about the intended meaning of the piece. It is, in short, a work of modern art. It is also a failure, in that it proves unequal to its declared purpose, which is emphatically communal. '*Dispersed are we; who have come together*', goes the gramophone at the end; '*let us retain whatever made that harmony*'. But there has been no harmony. The putative collective subjectivity of the audience has remained inchoate – 'orts and fragments', in the words of the pageant's narrator – and even the pious hope of 'unity' will be broken down to an abstract sign of negation: 'The gramophone gurgled *Unity-Dispersity*. It gurgled *Un … dis …* And ceased' (196, 201, italics original).

La Trobe is not only the maker of the pageant. Like an earlier female artist-figure of Woolf's, Lily Briscoe in *To the Lighthouse*, she is presented as if she were the artificer of the action she is a part of; her end-of-day vision anticipates that of the novel, as if she were taking command of its reality. But here again the point of the comparison is the contrast. Lily's creativity brings reso-lution of an old hurt; La Trobe's achieves only a glimpse of a beginning. Night comes, and Isa and Giles are left to themselves for the fight they cannot any longer postpone, in a landscape stripped of all social amenity, 'the heart of darkness'.[11] La Trobe has imagined the first words, but they will remain her secret; Woolf's narrative gives no access to them. 'Then the curtain rose. They spoke' (219). That is all.

3

Orlando narrates the exaltation of an 'infinitely noble' cultural subject capable of transcending the most basic of natural con-straints – sex and mortality – to resume and outdo all of English literature, the apotheosis of blue blood. In *Between the Acts*,

---

11   The allusion to Conrad is Woolf's.

Woolf was possessed by something like the opposite vision: an entropic downward movement into 'dispersity' leading to a general cultural involution. *Brideshead Revisited*, published just three years later, in 1945, united the two movements in a single narrative sequence, an Arcadian immersion in aristocratic life-as-art followed by a history of crisis and loss, all conveyed in the bleak recollections of a society painter, Charles Ryder. The retrospective narrative mode is essential to the suggestion of the novel. This is a *Bildungsroman*, but one whose story, itself some twenty years unfolding, has reached conclusion five years before the event that prompts its telling. Its irony is thus structural: hope and promise are remembered from somewhere on their other side – the Arcadian motif itself is given in the form of a disillusionment, in the classical funerary inscription that gives the first part of the novel its title, *Et in Arcadia ego*.

The social relations of the narrative are also established early. Of his first, unexpected visit to Brideshead Charles says: 'It was a glimpse only, such as might be had from the top of an omnibus into a lighted ballroom...' (39). His story involves a social passage upwards, and from outside to inside. The starting point is itself elevated: Charles is upper middle class, the son of a leisured antiquary (and thus, for relevant comparison, the equal of the Schlegels in means and social status). But if the class distance and the incline are not all that his yearning simile might suggest, they are real enough: the first thing we learn about Sebastian is that his family is aristocracy: his father is a marquess and his mother is descended from old Catholic gentry. And 'glimpse' fairly renders the experience of a fulfilment twice granted and twice taken away.

The passage is from one kind of cultural subjectivity to

another. The Charles Ryder who arrives in Oxford to read
History is academically inclined, inheriting something of his
father's disposition, and is soon 'adopted' by 'the college intellectuals', who pursue 'a middle course of culture', serious and
inquiring, between the 'flamboyant' aesthetes and 'the proletarian scholars who scramble fiercely for facts' (29). A year later he
has become an aesthete of a kind. The interest in art, and aptitude
for it, are unremarkable in themselves: they are among the givens
of his early life. What occurs now is a change in his perception
of art, a desegregation of aesthetic experience whose corollary is
an elective aestheticization of existence in general. The change
is identified, with emphasis, as consisting in a repudiation of
Bloomsbury aesthetics, represented by Roger Fry's painting and
Clive Bell's theory of 'significant form', and the inspiration in
both instances is Sebastian (35, 30). Art now finds its place in a
chain of associations and equivalents including cognate activities such as design and architecture, literature and also persons
and landscapes, whose ideal shared denominator is beauty – or,
in one of the novel's decisive terms, 'charm'. Oxford is 'a city
of aquatint'; Brideshead appears as a work in *grisaille*, and the
'exquisite man-made landscape' surrounding it is Keatsian. In
Charles's college rooms, Lalique glassware assumes the role first
taken by the painted screen or broadsheet poetry, along with
the Charvet tie that Sebastian borrows to set off his 'arresting'
beauty. Sebastian's given name comes with its own iconography,
as his fellow-undergraduate Anthony Blanche reminds him, and
his sister Julia, with her 'face of flawless *quattrocento* beauty',
quite simply is art (54). But art is not Julia's only metaphor, as
Charles makes plain in recalling their first sexual contact: 'It was
as though a deed of conveyance of her narrow loins had been

drawn and sealed. I was making my first entry as the freeholder of a property I would enjoy and develop at leisure' (248). From art to the sexual body to real estate: this desublimating sequence illuminates, in its brutal reverse, the normal direction of metaphoric flow, which is the opposite, and its purpose, which is best exemplified in the constant fetishizing of the architecture and décor of the great house. Brideshead is at the core of a tropology by which aristocracy is transfigured as style.

Two large questions govern the narrative of *Brideshead Revisited*. The first is the generic question of the *Bildungsroman* as such: what will become of young Charles Ryder? The second, which begins from quite distinct assumptions and has far wider significance but nevertheless becomes for a time a version of the first, is: what will become of Brideshead, the house and the line?

Brideshead, for Charles, is life-as-art: Baroque and fine wine flank his drawing and painting in a perfect ensemble during the long summer days alone with Sebastian. The idea of family attachment is present too, a lack in his own formation even if his friend experiences it as a choking surfeit – and here, inevitably, it is imprinted as lineage, as the necessary attribute of a social class. He carries the moral distillate of that time into his first exile from Brideshead, after he has abandoned Oxford – now sans Sebastian – for art school and Paris. One night he finds himself dining with Rex Mottram, the bourgeois adventurer from Canada who is engaged to be married to Julia. Dinner is on Mottram, of course, but Charles has chosen the restaurant and ordered the food and wine. Inwardly appalled by his host's crass monologues, he drifts away, comforted that 'the world was an older and better place than Rex knew, that mankind in its long passion had learned

another wisdom than his' (169). The cue for this is nothing more
mysterious than the Burgundy they are drinking, but the thought
has much wider application for Charles.[12] Within a few years,
thanks to a commission from Sebastian's father, he launches a
career as a memorialist of sorts, a portraitist of distinguished old
houses; he also marries the daughter of a viscount, Celia, who
brings him property, children and management services for his
work as a heritage painter. In him, the ideal union of art and aristocracy seems confirmed.

Counterpointing this progress towards fulfilment is the loss
of strength and coherence in the real aristocracy of Brideshead. Lady Marchmain, effectively the head of the family in
the absence of her self-exiled husband, falls ill and dies. Bridey,
the heir, remains undecided in everything except his unbending
Catholicism. Julia's marriage to Mottram is a threefold affront –
to religious and national pieties as well as social *point d'honneur*
– and before long a cause of misery to her. Sebastian, now in
Morocco, is an alcoholic wreck, and Cordelia, the youngest, is
an unworldly bride of Christ. Two unexpected developments
seem to alter the prospects for continuity at Brideshead. Charles
and Julia start an affair and eventually leave their respective
spouses, intending to marry. Soon afterwards, Bridey announces
his marriage to a widow of the middle class. The social ascription is crucial, as is the expectation that there will be no children.
Rex now leaves Brideshead; but contrary to plan, he will not be
succeeded by Beryl, Bridey's new wife. The Marquess, who has

---

12   The paragraph continues: 'By chance I met this same wine again,
lunching with my wine merchant in St James's Street, in the first autumn of
the war; it had softened and faded in the intervening years, but it still spoke in
the pure, authentic accent of its prime, the same words of hope.'

come home to die, is 'appalled' to think of her in his mother's place – 'Why should that uncouth pair sit here childless while the place crumbles about their ears?' (304) – and decides to leave the house to Julia. It is a decision made in the fullest consciousness of lineage:

> We were knights then, barons since Agincourt, the larger honours came with the Georges. They came the last and they'll go the first; the barony goes on. When all of you are dead Julia's son will be called by the name his fathers bore before the fat days; the days of wool shearing and the wide corn lands, the days of growth and building, when the marshes were drained and the waste land brought under the plough, when one built the house, his son added the dome, his son spread the wings and dammed the river... (317)

Julia inherits, but there will be no son. Overcome by her Catholic sense of sin, after her father's deathbed reconciliation with the Church, she decides she cannot be with Charles 'ever again'. Marchmain might be recalling a passage from *Orlando*, so close is it in feeling. But in *Brideshead*, in polar contrast to the miraculous outcome in Woolf's novel, it is as if the family extinguishes itself.

Charles's story might well be called 'Brideshead', but Waugh's novel is about Brideshead *revisited*, and thus, as he later wrote, 'a souvenir of the Second [World] War rather than of the twenties or of the thirties, with which it ostensibly deals'.[13] Set in 1943, after the turning-point of the war, the novel pictures a defining

---

13   'Preface' to the second, revised edition, 1960, p. 8.

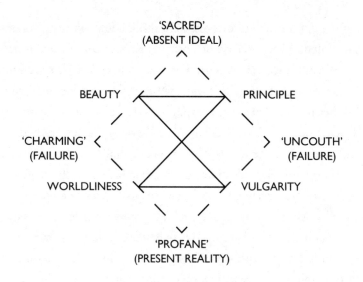

Figure 3 *Brideshead Revisited*

moment of transition from a valued past to an ominous future. Wartime duty has completed the dispersal of the family, and the house itself, requisitioned for use by the army, has been abused, as if humiliated. Where Mottram was in the end dismissed and Beryl's succession forestalled, a demotic conscript army has prevailed, in the exemplary figure of Captain Ryder's new subaltern, Hooper – who completes the semantic scheme of the narrative (Figure 3).

Beauty and *principle* are the competing master-values of the younger Flytes. Sebastian and Julia are beautiful but *worldly*, whereas their siblings, Bridey and Cordelia, are *principled* but plain. The fourth term of the square is *vulgarity*, which, as Charles's narrative opens, has no avatar, being simply the general negation of the world he moves in. Sebastian and Julia, to the left of the square, pursue worldly satisfactions, he cultivating a rarefied, escapist hedonism, she making a brilliant social début, then marrying Rex outside the rite of the Church (he is a divorcee). This narrative zone is also Charles's, and his fortunes bear out its general rule, which is that nothing ends well. Sebastian's anti-narrative compulsion – an infantile resistance to development – leads to alcoholic collapse. Julia suffers neglect and betrayal at the hands of a man she comes to regard as less than human. Charles's marriage likewise fails, and the prospect of a second marriage, to an heiress of even higher standing, is annulled with deadly finality. In the opposite zone of possibility, relatively little happens until Bridey decides to marry his 'uncouth' and penniless Catholic widow. This is the resolution of principle and vulgarity, and it brings failure of another kind: loss of the ancestral home and the ending of the male line.[14] At the upper vertex of the system, Lady Marchmain embodies in her person an existing, spontaneous union of beauty and principle. Her death marks the closing down of that 'sacred' possibility, which Julia's late reconversion cannot reopen. If she continues the family line, as her father hoped, it will be as a woman confirmed in mortal sin; the proof of her heartfelt purpose of amendment, contrariwise, will entail childlessness.

The sole remaining space of narrative possibility is that defined by worldliness and vulgarity. This is the banal world of the military rank and file: men once 'strong and hopeful' but soon demoralized by 'the smell of the fried-fish shops, ... familiar peace-time sounds of the works' siren and the dance-hall band', devoted to broadcast entertainment and beer (10–11). It is

---

14   Cordelia, for her part, will not marry, and Charles notes that her experience as a battlefield nurse in the Spanish Civil War has coarsened her – rendered her vulgar in another way.

the profane world of Hooper. Unromantic, barely competent, his mind permanently fog-bound, on the morning of his departure for Brideshead, in full kit, Hooper 'look[s] scarcely human' (15). This is one of several qualities he shares with Rex Mottram (who is by now a government minister), and his presence in the house, like Mottram's years before, is a historical portent:

> The builders did not know the uses to which their work would descend; they made a new house with the stones of the old castle; year by year, generation after generation, they enriched and extended it; year by year the great harvest of timber in the park grew to ripeness; until in sudden frost, came the age of Hooper; the place was desolate and the work all brought to nothing; *Quomodo sedet sola civitas* (330–1).

Thus Charles's vision corrects Marchmain's. The Flytes are passing, and Hooper will inherit. The end of aristocracy is not merely a break; it means ruin, and, as the biblical Latin suggests, Charles has despaired of human consolation.[15] He is, by his own account, 'homeless, childless, middle-aged, loveless', and about his art, which Anthony Blanche has dismissed as merely 'charming', he no longer has anything to say.[16] The displacement of class

---

15 Charles is echoing Cordelia, who was quoting the Vulgate Latin Bible, Lamentations 1:1. An English version reads: 'How doth the city sit solitary, that was full of people! How she is become as a widow!'

16 At p. 330. This devastating response to Charles's Latin American paintings (256–7) is the last word. Blanche, not English and possibly Jewish, an aesthete and homosexual, a self-described 'degenerate dago', is most obviously the antithesis of cousin Jasper – the nightmare come true. But he is more than that. With his combination of artistic commitments and unflinching critical candour, he belongs with Teresa Marchmain as a possible union of beauty

into art has now been doubled, in a further displacement from secular to religious culture. What remains is not of this world: it is the 'small red flame' of Catholic belief.

4

Still, even in this hopeless prevision of the post-war future, it is the practice of belief that takes the emphasis, not its metaphysical substance: a practice materialized in the symbolism, furnishings and 'old stones' of the private chapel at Brideshead. Waugh confirmed this fifteen years later, in his preface to the second, 1960 edition of the novel, which made passing mention – literary rather than theological – of mortal sin but gave a full, sanguine paragraph to 'the ancestral seats which were our chief national artistic achievement'. The English country house had not, after all, been vandalized by Hooper (and Labour). On the contrary, he wrote, it had unexpectedly become the object of a cult, and was now better cared for than it could have been by its aristocratic owners – who were themselves faring much better than he had expected (8). In fact, as he may have been aware, the cult had been announced years before, and assigned its general legitimating purpose, on the occasion of the transfer of Orlando's home to the National Trust in 1947. Knole, in the county of Kent, was the seat of the Sackvilles, Earls of Dorset, and, as Vita Sackville-West confirmed in an article she wrote for the London *Spectator* at the time, the original of the house that Woolf had celebrated in *Orlando*. Its significance – the significance of all such places – was that

---

and principle. As such, he embodies and speaks a radical, *maudit* alternative to the moral order of Brideshead.

In times when the esteem of beauty and the humanities hides like an unhonoured nymph from the eyes of men; times when expediency, convenience, and economy demand our entire and sole consideration; ... times when beauty and all that stands for culture make no more impact on men's ears than the unreality of a dead language – in such times it comes as a plumb luxury to indulge even for a moment in the contemplation of something so very different, something so unnecessary, so inordinate, prodigal, extravagant, and traditional, as the great houses of the past.

Yet they grew organically, as Woolf had perceived, thus 'put[ting] her fingers on the still living truth of this massive anachronism'; and for the solace of the generations who made such houses, Sackville-West continued,

> let us suggest that some grace of another age may seep into the consciousness of the million wandering freely among these ancient courts, and that the new young Richards, Johns, Annes and Elizabeths ... may find enrichment in the gift of something so old, so courteous, and so lovely.

Here is a Burkean vision of English continuity, a vision of aristocracy as literature and culture such as Woolf had sponsored in *Orlando* (and Sackville-West before her, in her book *Knole and the Sackvilles*), now rendered programmatic as a spiritual education for the popular millions of post-war Britain.[17]

---

17   Vita Sackville-West, *Knole and the Sackvilles*, third edition, Tonbridge, 1949, appendix 2, pp. 215–18. The relationship between Knole and *Orlando* was inferred from earliest days; that between Woolf's novel and this family history, which was first published in 1922, six years before *Orlando*, calls for emphasis.

3. *The Horror* ...

But what were the millions that might visit Knole in 'the days of democracy', and what might they make of its offering of grace?

In Jude Fawley and Leonard Bast, both ambiguous creations, the fervour of self-education readily turns a little absurd; the quest for culture is ill-conceived and prone to accidents, exposing its plebeian heroes as figures of fun or pathos. Yet for all the ambivalence that went into their imagining, they are in no way malign, never represented as endangering the culture they seek access to: Jude goes on repairing the walls that exclude him, and in Wickham Place Bast's goblin footfall comes as a moral challenge, not a menace. The sense of threat is present in Woolf, but its provenance is middle class – the entrepreneurial writer and the earnest middlebrow – not the servants and all their kind, who are a version of pastoral, good-hearted complements of their natural superiors. It is with *Brideshead Revisited* that a new and ominous popular subject comes in view, acquiring the momentum of historical process, as representative of a new cultural order. Waugh's 'Age of Hooper' is socially under-defined, but certainly low in general aspect; it names the coming ascendancy of those too unlike to be responsive to older ways yet now too close and too confident to be checked in their claim to entitlement; it enshrines the self-contradiction in bien-pensant notions of cultural progress.

I

Just three years after *Brideshead*, in 1948, Elizabeth Bowen published *The Heat of the Day*, another narrative of Britain in wartime including a mordant figuration of the new popular cultural subject. There is nothing of Hooper's indefinite demotic in Louie Lewis: she is a factory worker, married to an electrician, Tom, who is now serving in North Africa. She has no grasp of temporal order, no internal censor, and no spontaneous feel for what she is or ought to be. In her present circumstances she is sexually promiscuous, for the paradoxical reason that 'she felt nearer Tom with any man than she did with no man'. Lacking his guidance, 'she look[s] about her in vain for someone to imitate'.[1] The newspapers are her salvation. It is not the news that commands her attention (she lacks the general knowledge she would need to interpret the war reports) but 'the ideas', the inspirational articles that interpellate her, introduce her to the selves she now sees she is, and confirm her as a person in good standing: 'Was she not a worker, a soldier's lonely wife, a war orphan, a pedestrian, a Londoner, a home- and animal-lover, a thinking democrat, a movie-goer, a woman of Britain, a letter-writer, a

---

1   Elizabeth Bowen, *The Heat of the Day* (1948), London, 1998, pp. 145, 15. Further page references appear in brackets in the main text.

fuel-saver and a housewife?' Thus, in the wartime press, Louie 'finds peace' (151–2).

The greater part of Bowen's novel is devoted to the story of another, entirely different woman, the upper-middle-class Stella Rodney, and in this perspective the newspaper sequence, a duologue between Louie and her more sceptical fellow-reader, Connie, can be seen as a comic interlude. At the centre of Stella's narrative are questions of property: the Anglo-Irish estate that has unexpectedly passed to her son, though with what practical prospects it is too early to say; in contrast, if it is entirely a contrast, her own vagrant moves from one flat to another – and all this caught in the eldritch light of London in 1944. Yet it is Louie's story that opens and closes the novel, in this way defining the historical ground of Stella's unsettled, parenthetical existence. The Allied reinvasion of Europe has begun at last, bringing Louie some crucial personal good luck: Tom dies on the Italian front, just too soon to catch the revelation of his wife's reckless pregnancy. Months later, after the D-Day landings, Louie has begun her new life as an 'orderly mother'. Out airing her baby, whose name is Tom Victor, she catches sight of a movement overhead and holds him aloft, 'hoping he too might see, and perhaps remember. Three swans were flying a straight flight. They passed overhead, disappearing in the direction of the west' (330). At that the novel ends, with Louie's triumph and, little though she knows it, an image that might be from Yeats, the iconographer of the Anglo-Irish gentry to which Bowen herself belonged, suggesting impermanence, and the waning of an older order of things.[2]

---

2   See, for Bowen's biographical context and relevant comparisons with *Orlando* and *Brideshead Revisited*, her family history *Bowen's Court & Seven*

Between Bowen's Louie Lewis and Ingrid Rothwell in Stan Barstow's *A Kind of Loving* there elapsed something more than a decade, a span of years in which the institutional foundations of British culture in the later twentieth century were decisively configured. Liberal paternalism and democratic demand combined to create the ensemble of 'the welfare state' – a national health service, social security and universal secondary education. The long economic boom, with high levels of employment, facilitated the rapid expansion of markets in consumer durables and underwrote the credit schemes that financed the newly 'affluent' working class, which was still an overwhelming majority in the population. The cultural capstone of the new order was Britain's bimodal television system, in one part public-service in constitution, as the national broadcasting organization had been since its beginnings in the 1920s, but now – from 1955 – with a new sector funded through commercial advertising. *A Kind of Loving* offered a conspectus of this emerging culture, seen through the eyes of another, slightly older Victor, twenty-year-old Vic Brown, a West Yorkshire coal-miner's son, whose *Bildung* occupies the foreground of the novel.

The narrative is Vic's, a personal present-tense account of two years in which he sets out to win the affections of a pretty workplace colleague, Ingrid, succeeding only too fully, and ending up married in haste to a woman whose loving feelings he cannot return. It is also, for him, a period of cultural uncertainty, as he considers the range now available to him, whether through the settled examples of family, friends and workmates, or through new, unexpected opportunities; alone among the

---

Winters (both 1942), London, 1984, and especially the 'Afterword', dated 1963, with its elegiac reflections on her class, esp. 455–9.

people he knows, he has yet to make his choices. The cultural landscape in which he moves is markedly modern in texture. The younger Browns are all grammar-school products, and upwardly mobile; Vic's Saturday job is in a shop selling televisions and record players; some coal-miners now drive their own cars to work; among the fashionable younger generation, America is a byword. This is not the levelled world of 'mass civilization', however: the reading preferences in the factory drawing office where Vic works include the *Manchester Guardian* as well as the *Daily Mirror*, the sporting press and *Snappy Nudes*; cinema choices include an art-house adaptation from Zola as well as the new Burt Lancaster. The novel emphasizes the variety and uncertainty of such choices. Older cultural formations persist: Vic's father plays in a brass band, while his Saturday employer and patron is devoted to classical music; institutional Christianity is still present; trade-unionism and Labour remain touchstones of social identity. Above all, as a governing last instance, framing the possibilities of individual disposition and movement, there is the communal ethos whose crowning metonym is 'family'. So it is that the novel opens the day after Christmas with Vic's sister's wedding, and ends as he resolves to make the best of his own ill-assorted union, with another Christmas just weeks away.

The mismatch is cultural. Vic is no 'Highbrow' – a term that belongs to the common vocabulary of his home town – but he is thoughtful, intellectually undefensive, and more and more drawn to classical music, whereas Ingrid has grown up with a mother who declares that her daughter 'knows what she likes and … doesn't pretend to enjoy highbrow nonsense'. (She owes her name itself to her mother's Hollywood heroine.) Vic is fond of reading, which he prefers to television, and his new brother-in-law is encouraging him towards more ambitious material, but Ingrid – 'Good heavens, no, she says, she can't read books. She gets three magazines a week and can hardly get through them for watching telly', which, here and from now on in this tradition, is the key index of cultural inanition and worse.[3] Vic has fallen for Ingrid's looks and sexual promise, and fancied that he loves her, but soon realizes that

> I don't love her, and that's the awful truth. I don't even like her much now. ... I wonder how I've stood it as long as I have: her gossip and silly scandal and quiz shows and every little detail about how some lucky housewife from Wolverhampton or Tooting won a refrigerator or three thousand pairs of nylons and a holiday in America by answering questions you'd have got your arse tanned if you didn't know the answers to in Standard Four. ... I just don't understand it. I don't understand it at all.[4]

But Ingrid is pregnant and the communal code of honour dictates his course: he must marry her and endure a life sentence with someone who will not share his books or his music. Modest though Vic's cultural aspirations may be, Ingrid can only prove a hindrance to him, even if he learns 'a kind of loving', for there is no suggestion from any quarter that Ingrid might change. Demanding cultural interests, in this world, are for men. (Even Vic's sister Chris, the teacher, who is her brother's model of a perfect companion, rations the exercise of her educated capabilities: she is aware of what lies inside the covers of her husband's copy of *Ulysses*, but sees no need for first-hand acquaintance

---

3 Stan Barstow, *A Kind of Loving* (1960), Cardigan, 2010, pp. 281, 128.
4 Ibid., pp. 156–7.

with it.) Ingrid is more sympathetically imagined than her sister-figures in this genre, but they are sisters none the less, forming a developing sequence from a state of cultural nature to the full franchise of the mass market: Arabella and Jackie, the unculturable encumbrances of imperfect men who deserved higher things; closer in time and historical type, Louie, the subjective blank given her sense of herself only by the inscriptions of the press; and now another snare like Arabella, as passive in her way as Louie – Ingrid, the pretty, empty-headed consumer of cultural trash.

2

– Once I let myself dream I hit her across the face as I saw it done once by a chap in a telly play. Perhaps that was when it all started.

– Such people. I must have stood next to them in the Tube, passed them in the street, of course I've overheard them and I knew they existed. But never really believed they exist. So totally blind.

Fred Clegg, an office clerk and amateur entomologist, has made a socially contrasting choice of love-object, becoming infatuated with Miranda Gray, a beautiful, clever art student from a professional middle-class home. A massive win on the football pools transforms his sense of possibility, soon tipping his obsessive daydream into psychosis, and he kidnaps her as his special

The Horror ...

'guest' and companion-to-be. The significance of the encounter between Fred and Miranda is the substance of John Fowles's thriller *The Collector*.[5]

The first of the two personal narratives that make up the novel is Fred's; the second, which he will eventually discover and read, is Miranda's diary of her captivity in the cellar of the remote cottage he has bought for the purpose. The relationship between these narratives is one between knowledges, in part the inevitably discrepant bodies of knowledge of two individuals with no prior acquaintance, but more importantly the different orders in a hierarchy of cultural knowledge. Fred's narrative is retrospective and temporally complete; it englobes Miranda's and in that basic sense offers a meta-discourse. But Miranda knows much more, about many things, including the irony of his affecting the name Ferdinand, in ignorance of *The Tempest* and therefore of Prospero's daughter – and of Caliban, whose name she gives him instead. Miranda is well versed in literature, art, music and politics and thus Fred's cultural superior. However, she in turn defers to the artist G.P., a friend and mentor much older than her, and a recurring presence in her journal:

> The old Eve takes over [says G.P., who is holding forth, in his fashion, about women]. Exit Anadyomene.
> Who's she, I asked.
> He explained. ...
> After a while he said, you've read Jung?
> No, I said.

5   John Fowles, *The Collector* (1963), London, 1989. The opening quotations are from Fred (p. 11) and Miranda (p. 148) respectively. Further page references appear in brackets in the main text.

He's given your species of the sex a name. Not that it helps.
The disease is just as bad.

Tell me the name, I said.

He said, you don't tell diseases their names. (176)

This exchange dramatizes the upper levels of the novel's cultural hierarchy. G.P. grants Miranda a fragment of knowledge, which she receives and stores.[6] A little later, then, he will withhold another fragment, as a move in the psychodrama of their relationship, and what there is to be told remains unknown. G.P. is, at such moments, externally focalized, a character who is more knowledgeable than his narrator and thus senior in the hierarchy of the narrative to Miranda herself. However, even he is not paramount. There is another relationship to note, also strongly marked. The meaning of the name Anadyomene would be lost on Fred, and Miranda is ignorant of the name Jung has given her 'species' of female. But the reader may be similarly disadvantaged, here and elsewhere in the novel, and this knowledge differential will not be equalized: it remains as a sign of itself, an index of cultural inequality.

The prime instance of this rhetoric is the unidentified fragment of text that presides over the fiction as a whole, announcing an unconditional meta-discourse, in a language that none of the characters and few of the readers understand: *que fors aus ne le sot riens nee*. The words come from a thirteenth-century Burgundian poem, *La Châtelaine de Vergi*, and their English meaning is, roughly, 'besides them no one knew anything'.[7] 'They' are the lady of the

---

6   G.P. stands for George Paston. See p. 135 below.

7   It is only proper, in the circumstances, to declare that I owe this information to a Google search.

title and her knightly lover, and there is little in their story that associates them with the antithetical relationship between Fred and Miranda except that in both cases the man brings about the death of the woman: the lady dies on discovering that her lover has broken their pact of silence, while Miranda is condemned by secrecy. The secrecy is a necessary concomitant of the abduction, but the unknowns of Fowles's novel include much more than the particulars of a crime. The criminal form of the encounter between the two, by association, lends colour and drama to its social and cultural substance, which thus becomes a secret of another kind. 'If only they knew', Miranda writes. 'If only *they* knew' (117). The stress on knowledge is already noteworthy, but then, on hearing the sound of an aeroplane overhead, she says:

> If only people knew what they flew over.
> We're all in aeroplanes. (126)

The metaphoric outgrowth of the second sentence confirms the generalizing potential of 'people' and what they, now 'we', should know but do not. This mounting emphasis on the unknown, in Miranda and G.P. and, beyond all irony, in John Fowles himself, licenses the essential conceit of the novel, which is *revelation*, and what is to be revealed is the truth of the contemporary social order of culture.

The encounter, to begin with, is entirely of Fred's design, which is conceived in the terms of his pastime. Miranda, 'elusive, sporadic, and very refined', is 'not like the other ones, even the pretty ones. More for the real connoisseur' (9). Just seeing her is like 'catching a rarity', as if recognition and possession were one and the same. Now, thanks to his big win, they can be. ('That's the thing about money. There are no obstacles.') He can never get to know Miranda 'in the ordinary way', but, once with him, 'captive' but 'in a nice way', 'she'll see my good points, she'll understand. There was always the idea she would understand' (19). What ensues, in fact, is a psycho-social struggle of a kind, in which Miranda deploys her considerable cultural capital in successive attempts to soothe, distract, outwit, undermine, humiliate or even redeem this man in whom she sees not merely a deadly personal threat but a living offence against her intuitions of authentic judgement in art, ideas and manners. Immediately noting that 'he has one of those funny inbetween voices, uneducated trying to be educated' (122), she wages war on his speech: 'One day I remember she said, "You know what you do? You know how rain takes the colour out of everything? That's what you do to the English language. You blur it every time you open your mouth"' (67). In particular, she mocks his genteelisms, in which until now he has taken some pride:

Why do you keep on using these stupid words – nasty, nice, proper, right? Why are you worried about what's proper? You're like a little old maid who thinks marriage is dirty and everything except cups of weak tea in a stuffy old room is dirty. Why do you take all the life out of life? Why do you kill all the beauty? (75–6)

– This after she has smashed the commonplace knick-knacks, 'the monsters', he has chosen to decorate the 'lounge' of his seventeenth-century cottage.

'The idea' on which Fred was depending has come to nothing, and in response to his 'bossy' captive, with her 'la-di-da' ways and cleverness, he falls back on the one thing he knows he can still assert with confidence and point: the continuing reality of class-cultural subordination.

> C[aliban].[8] It's the one thing you don't understand. You only got to walk into a room, people like you, and you can talk with anyone, you understand things, but when …
>
> M. *Do* shut up. You're ugly enough without starting to whine.
> (186)

Fred has offered his narrative of their situation: his love for her. She proposes counter-narratives: they are in a version of *Beauty and the Beast*, and he can redeem himself only by letting her go; or he is a character in her cartoon strip, 'The Awful Tale of a Harmless Boy': 'Absurd. But I have to keep the reality and the horror at bay. He starts by being a nice little clerk and ends up as a drooling horror-film monster' (203).

If Fred is a psychotic Bast, Miranda is typologically a Schlegel – Helen rather than Margaret. Her efforts to interest him in jazz and samba, or art history and drawing, are in part tactical initiatives, but also responses to the sadness she sees in him; at times she is conscious of a destiny shared, even if unwanted on her side; her attempt to seduce him is itself an inward protest at the 'inhumanity' of their situation, an acknowledgement of the standing injunction *Only connect*. Like *Howards End*, Fowles's novel is designedly a work of engaged cultural criticism.

It is a great convenience of personal narrative as a formal variety that it allows easy modulation between story-telling

---

8   See p. 10 above.

proper and essayistic modes such as generalized description, reflection and argument while honouring the established literary value of fluency. Thus, Miranda's diary is a record of her imprisonment and a reflection on the growth of her friendship with the charismatic bohemian G.P., and in both aspects the occasion for trenchant digressions on the order and social dynamics of British culture circa 1960. Miranda has come to understand that she, like G.P., is one of 'the Few', 'a sort of band of people who have to stand against all the rest', who have 'fought for the right things and created and painted in the right way, ... who don't lie about things, who try not to be lazy, who try to be human and intelligent. Yes, people like G.P., for all his faults' (208) – or like Matthew Arnold's 'best selves', to mark a pertinent resemblance from the 1860s. However, Miranda's reactions to 'the rest' outdo the most intemperate pages of *Culture and Anarchy*: 'I hate the uneducated and the ignorant. I hate the pompous and the phoney. I hate the jealous and the resentful. I hate the crabbed and the mean and the petty. I hate all ordinary dull little people who aren't ashamed of being dull and little' (207). The catalogue is as timeless as it is phobic, but there is historical specification to come:

> I hate what G.P. calls the New People, the new-class people with their cars and their money and their tellies and their stupid vulgarities and their stupid crawling imitation of the bourgeoisie. ... this awful dead weight of the fat little New People on everything. Corrupting everything. Vulgarizing everything. ... Everything mass-produced. Mass-everything. (207)

Miranda follows convention in insisting that her cultural categories are not simply to be mapped onto basic social classes: the

Few can be found anywhere in society, as of course can 'the rest'. But customary philistinism (such as she sees in her middle-class family) and the clumsiness and defensiveness born of heredi- tary subordination (Fred's lot) can hardly be represented as true equivalents in the sociology of culture. The perceived threat is a new one, socially quite specific, and it is on the move. These New People, 'the moneyed masses', are the creation of the Labour Party, says G.P, in another of his provocations, tacitly conflat- ing the post-war welfare reforms with the consumer boom that came a decade later. They embody 'affluence' without 'soul', and advance by luck rather than merit. Fred's 'fabulous' pools win is popular affluence exaggerated to the point of monstrosity, a condition already manifest in his speech and physical appear- ance, with unthinkable outcomes. Miranda, the clever, cultivated bourgeoise whose striking good looks are admired by all, fears she may be a 'martyr' of the resistance. Their relationship is a paranoid allegory of the whole culture, the dark truth of it, in years of significant expansion and change:

> It's like being in a city and being besieged. They're all around. And we've got to hold out.
>   It's a battle between Caliban and myself. He is the New People and I am the Few. (231)[9]

Miranda loses the battle, dying of pneumonia in her underground cell, and Fred learns a lesson from his struggle with her. In choos- ing as he did, he had over-reached himself socially; next time,

---

9   This passage comes from Miranda's critical discussion of Alan Sil- litoe's *Saturday Night and Sunday Morning*, which had appeared five years before *The Collector*.

he will stay closer to home. He has someone in mind already: 'an ordinary common shop-girl', someone who would 'respect' him, knowing 'who's boss', someone he could teach (282–3). It sounds like a new cultural order in miniature.

3

The Collector moves towards the disclosure of a state of cultural emergency. Of course there is no categorical suggestion that Fred Clegg is typical of his class – even if he reaches this conclusion himself, as he takes stock of Miranda's responses to him. Yet it is he, not his office colleagues, let alone a Vic Brown, who wins the pools and offers the live demonstration that popular aspiration plus opportunity means danger for the cultured few. In Ruth Rendell's *A Judgement in Stone*, the danger is in all respects closer to home. Appearing fourteen years after Fowles's, this novel emerged in quite distinct, more polarized cultural and political conditions. *The Collector*, like *A Kind of Loving*, was a moment in a continuing discourse on working-class 'affluence', in the closing days of a long stretch of Conservative rule in Britain. By 1977, when Rendell's novel appeared, Labour had been in office for ten of those years altogether, much of the time struggling to contain the militancy of the trade unions, which had brought down a Conservative government and would eventually launch the winter strike wave that settled the fate of Labour in the general election two years later. Resonating in an international context in which the appeal, or threat, of socialism seemed greater than at any time since the 1930s, these were among the general shaping conditions of Rendell's return to the topic of culture and classes.

A lot is established in the novel's first, tautly summarizing sentence: 'Eunice Parchman killed the Coverdale family because she could not read and write.'[10] Flouting a cardinal convention of so much crime writing, it is as revealing of the rhetoric as of the action to come. Unlike, say, *A Kind of Loving*, in which a personal narration couched in the present tense favours the suggestion of uncertainty, Rendell's narrative is non-focalized, 'omniscient', moving freely through the infinite space-time of the fiction, and with a temporality strongly marked by anticipation. The effect of this rhetorical combination, already tangible in this opening statement, is to lend prolepsis the air of report, as if in a forensics of the future. Once again, the letter killeth, and this time, it seems, as a matter of cultural fate: 'Had they been a family of philistines, they might be alive today ...' (7).

As it is, George and Jacqueline Coverdale are 'peculiarly literate' in background and habit, as are the children, one studying English at a nearby university, the other a farouche teenager with a taste for profundity. If their home, Lowfield Hall, has no space called a 'library' it is in part because the entire house is a reading room. However, there is nothing of the Schlegels' critical curiosity in this. The Coverdales' literary engagements are in the first place companionate, and Jackie makes a point of reading 'every new novel of note'. This is effort finely measured: culture without reduction but also without risk, that still point of civilized being known as cultivation. Above all, the Coverdales are true to their social type, as the narrative promptly reports, here again in one brisk sentence: 'The family belonged to the upper middle class, and they lived a conventional upper-middle-class life in a

---

10   Ruth Rendell, *A Judgement in Stone* (1977), London, 1978, p. 7. Further page references appear in brackets in the main text.

country house' (7). Specifically, George fulfils the English class ideal of the country-dwelling bourgeois. He is a Suffolk factory-owner who has made the transition from suburban villa to village manor house and assumed a social identity to match, he and Jacqueline 'in an unobtrusive way slipping into playing the parts of the squire and his lady' (8).[11] George's paternalism and Jacqueline's 'mighty airs' do not impress the network of families who make up the local popular classes, the Higgses, Meadowses, Baalhams and Newsteads. Eva Baalham, the slapdash cleaning lady, takes pride in her inherited distinction:

> In her eyes, the only difference between herself and the Cover-dales was one of money. In other respects she was their superior since they were newcomers and not even gentry but in trade, while her yeomen ancestors had lived in Greeving for five hundred years. (20–1)

This is the existing social order of the village as the novel opens, and fantasy is inherent in it. The lady of Lowfield Hall is married to 'the owner of a tin-can factory', after all, and if some of Eva's ancient yeoman connection are still in farming, another makes a living selling televisions – 'off the back of a lorry', as she suspects. Heritage is in the one case an affectation, in the other very likely just an old story, and either way insecure. Just how insecure is revealed when Jacqueline, despairing of the local domestics, advertises in the London *Times*. Hoping if not quite for 'someone like ourselves' then 'a reasonably educated person ... willing to take on domestic service for the sake of a nice home', she finds Eunice Parchman (10).

---

11   Grammar modified for context.

Eunice is a working-class Londoner, not at all like the Cover-dales and not much more like the Greeving locals. She has obtained her new position by false pretences, and has other, graver secrets to hide. But the secret that matters most to her, the one at the same time most shaming and most vulnerable to discovery, is that, far from being 'reasonably educated', she is illiterate – a fathomless human alienation, as the narrative insists. She has come to Lowfield in the hope of hiding her illiteracy from the world, at first with success beyond her expectation: the Coverdales even give her a television of her own, on which she watches her first violent crime drama. But everyday circum-stances bring suspicions, evasions and near misses. George and his daughter Melinda, both compulsive 'interferers', pester her with well-meaning help, such as the offer of an eye test, and Melinda at length chances upon the reality, triggering the crisis that leads to Eunice's dismissal (for threatening conduct) and, soon, to the massacre of the Coverdale family.

Her accomplice in this is Joan Smith, another Londoner, petty-bourgeois, with secrets in her past, and now running the village post office with her husband. She parallels Eunice in these ways, but is in one critical respect her opposite. An able pupil in her school days, she was a precocious reader and has remained a keen and curious one, supplementing her basic diet of religious tracts with her neighbours' incoming mail, both of which feed her growing paranoia. Whereas Eunice is unable to read what she must (a shopping list or a recipe), Joan hyper-actively reads what by law she must not. In her, the habit of reading is exorbitant and criminal. It is this pairing of psycho-cultural opposites that brings about the destruction of the Coverdales.

The destruction has representative significance, most evidently in general social terms. The murders are saturated with the indices of class, even in the practical detail of the event, in which the weapons of a gentleman (George's sporting guns) are turned against him by a disgraced employee and a trespasser. The desolation they bring about is quite general, as the narrative insists in its exhaustive itemizing of the consequences for the entire cast of the novel. The end of the family is the end of the way of life whose sacred token was the house, now abandoned because of an unresolvable testamentary crux. Where Orlando won, George's surviving children lose. The continuity the house has embodied is social and, specifically, literary. Lowfield is itself made out of literature, taking its name from *Jane Eyre*; Shakespeare is at hand to mourn its passing ('Bare ruined choirs…'), and Dickens to deplore the insanity of it all, in the bitter litany of nonsense from *Bleak House*. Still more than cultivation is at stake in this disaster, however, for it was a Coverdale who made the so-called Great Bible of 1540. Religious disposition is a systematic index in *A Judgement in Stone*, identifying each of the main characters according to a supreme code of evaluative suggestion. George and Jacqueline, conventional in this as in all things, are church-goers. Young Giles, who has been reading *Brideshead Revisited*, is undecided between Buddhism and Catholicism in the Oxford manner, while Melinda wrestles with *Sir Gawain*, a pagan poem by a Christian author. Eunice's father had read the Bible in its entirety, and in this way embodied cultural continuity with the historic Miles Coverdale; his daughter cancels this inheritance as matter-of-factly as she has ended his life. The only devout Christian in the story is Joan, the crazed sectarian herald of a second Epiphany.

Joan's madness is only partly a realist plot feature underwriting the development of commonplace social resentment into multiple homicide. It belongs with her past, which has been a serial scandal, and her appearance, which is frightful, outdoing Jacky Bast and Louie Lewis in its grotesquerie, in a strategy of pejoration that adds layer upon layer of antipathetic association to a character already positioned as a negative. The effect is still more marked in the case of Eunice, whose history includes blackmail and patricide, and whose appearance, though not alarming like Joan's, is odd, showing poorly in the company of the notably good-looking Coverdales. A 'housekeeper' of all incongruous things, Eunice is *unheimlich*, an uncanny chill at the heart of domestic conviviality. She is psychically alien: 'free in her mysterious dark freedom of sensation and instinct and blank absence of the printed word', she is deformed, a freak of civilization, and perhaps not quite human at all, rather an 'atavistic ape disguised as twentieth-century woman' (7). Such insistent overwriting prompts a cool return to the characters who excite it, the railway worker's illiterate daughter and the gifted schoolgirl who abandoned a good home for life on the other side, and to the metaphorical politics of their dealings with Greeving's squirearchical bourgeoisie. George Coverdale's habitual paternalism works in his factory and the villagers put up with it, though even in these peaceable settings there are indications that his interventions are defective: ill-judged, not helped by his wife's more prickly class demeanour, and anyway lacking customary legitimacy. But with the housekeeper and the postmistress, it does not work at all. Helpful offers of subsidized driving lessons and eye tests are simply threats to Eunice, whose paramount desire is to be left alone with her television and chocolates. George's status is likewise a provocation to Joan Smith, who has taken the weapons of Christianity and sharpened them for war on sociable Anglicans like himself. Here is a formula for disaster, as recognizable in its way as Fowles's. In *The Collector*, it was 'the moneyed masses' – popular aspiration fuelled by opportunity – that spelled cultural ruin. Now, it is the union of mindless workers with intellectuals gone to the bad. The horror circa 1960 was Labour; by the mid-1970s it was a prospect of socialist revolution.[12]

---

12   There is a light suggestion of this in Claude Chabrol's film adaptation of Rendell's novel, *La cérémonie* (1995). The difference is that Chabrol's duo are playing at *soixante-huitardes*, unlike their originals, who are entirely themselves, not borrowing from any precedent.

4. End-States

As it turned out, Rendell's novel was the Minerva's owl of middle-class alarmism. The great strike wave that cleared Margaret Thatcher's path to office was the last of its kind, and the sequence of industrial class battles that marked the first years of the new decade ended in the historic defeat of the miners' union in 1984–1985. The presiding caricatures of the new period, succeeding the phobic imagery of militant workers, belonged to an allegory of financial greed – appetite unbound in the neo-liberal order now emerging in the North Atlantic. Among the earliest of the many English avatars of such figures was the militantly uncouth John Self, protagonist of Martin Amis's *Money*.

I

'I hate people with degrees, O-levels, eleven-pluses, Iowa Tests, shorthand diplomas ...', Self declares. And, he continues,

And you hate me, don't you. Yes you do. Because I'm the new kind, the kind who has money but can never use it for anything but ugliness. To which I say: You never let us in, not really. You might have thought you let us in, but you never did. You just gave us some money.

And told us to get lost...[1]

In this way, *Money* reiterates and confirms the apprehensions of *The Collector*. However, although the theme and even the phrasings are familiar from Miranda and Fred, the hour is much later. The novels belong to distinct periods. Miranda is, literally enough, a daughter of the National Health Service, and in Fred something of the old working-class will to education persists, even if in a weak and misshapen form. John Self, in hyperbolic contrast, buys his dental care for cash in the medical black economy, and is aggressively philistine both in his work in advertising and in his personal life. In his own summation, he is a 'yob'.

Textually, Self is a voice: *Money* is from beginning to end an address. His desires having come to nothing or worse – his film-making ambitions have led to ruin, not riches, and the two women in his life have left him – he is writing a suicide note, to whom is not quite clear, even though the short-list of likely addressees is short indeed, and certainly includes the likes of 'you', the reader of so-called literary novels. The substance of the narrative is the elaboration of this speaking subject and the environment that sustains it. What happens in the course of this

---

1   Martin Amis, *Money: A Suicide Note* (1984), London, 2005, p. 58. Further page references appear in brackets in the main text.

is by way of illustration only, a set of non-events in a closed historical situation.

Older markers of nationality and class do not quite capture Self's identity. The child of English and American parents, he has grown up partly in New Jersey and partly in a London pub called the Shakespeare, now speaking a demotic that mixes US and British English slang. Nearly if not quite working class by origin, he has risen to become a partner in a successful advertising firm, well-off, and mobile to the point of rootlessness: his apartment and everything in it are rented; only his car is his own. Hardly bourgeois either, in any received sense, he is a condensed social figure, a plebeian with the reflexes of a street tough and pockets full of money. In him, mobility appears as degradation. Self is above all a force of consumption, by his own avowal 'addicted to the twentieth century'; he gorges himself unceasingly on a late-century cocktail of alcohol, tobacco, drugs, pornography and junk food. Money is the shared denominator of these things, and of his personal relations with others – Alec, who uses him as a free overdraft facility; Barry, his purported father, who has billed him for the expenses of his upbringing; and Selina, the expensive girlfriend whose auto-pornographic routines are the climax of gluttonous evenings on the town. *Money* the novel is satire in the prophetic spirit – *radix malorum est cupiditas*[2] – and the bright lights of the town, London or New York indifferently, display the truth of the situation it excoriates, parading the familiar names and titles of classic literature everywhere – stay at the Carraway, eat at Kreutzer's, drink Desdemona Cream and, for those anxious moments, take a Serafim – but with not a book in

---

2 Or 'Greed is the root of all evil', 1 Timothy 6:10.

sight or in mind. The film industry, the main stage of the novel, is a waste of fantasists and cynics; 'creativity' is now the pretension of strippers. Culture has been prostituted wholesale and therewith annulled as a means of transcendence.

Elements of an older order survive. Selina's boyfriend may be her john, but the aim of her manipulation and deceit is marriage and motherhood; Fat Vince, the factotum at the Shakespeare – and, it will emerge, Self's natural father – remains loyal to 'real food', roll-mops, tripe and brains; and even Self owns up to missing the local Italian family restaurant, which has been replaced by yet another burger franchise. But these feelings are like keepsakes. The only conceivable counter-force in Self's life is his old friend from film school, Martina, who seems to him ineffable:

> The thing about Martina is – the thing about Martina is I can't find a voice to summon her with. The voices of money, weather and pornography (all that uncontrollable stuff), they just aren't up to the job when it comes to Martina. I think of her and there is a speechless upheaval in me – I feel like this when I'm in Zurich, Frankfurt or Paris and the locals can't speak the lingo. My tongue moves in search of patterns and grids that simply are not there. Then I shout... (119)

Martina is in every way Self's antitype. Reversing the pattern of his youth, she is an American raised in England. Where he is brash, flash and boorish, she is refined. In these respects, Martina is his girlfriend's opposite too, though even Selina is envious of her sexual appeal: 'You think she's the cat's miaow, don't you [she sneers at John], with her degrees and her big arse' (89).

Above all, whereas Self and Selina represent the newest of new money, and the degrading means of amassing it, the thing about Martina is that 'she has never not had money' (her Manhattan townhouse is on Bank Street), known the strain of the lack of it:

> Her smile is knowing, roused and playful, but also innocent, because money makes you innocent when it's been there all along. How else can you hang out on this planet for thirty years while still remaining free? Martina is not a woman of the world. She is a woman of somewhere else. (134)

This somewhere else is the conventional world of modern literature, music and art, and Self is willing to join Martina in it, as she is to induct him. But the effort of redemption is thwarted by Selina, who tricks Self into a final pornographic scenario with the aim of repelling its unsuspecting witness, Martina. The scheme works, and the door to somewhere else shuts tight, leaving Self alone in his familiar circuit of commodified excess.

As allegory, Martina's rout signifies the futility of the old cultural paternalism: even if one yob is ready to change, there will be another to block the attempt, as if to reassert a fundamental difference of kind:

> 'I wouldn't want you to be happy with anyone else. And not with her. What did she see in you anyway?'
> 'I don't know.'
> … 'Would she have made you happy?'
> 'I don't know.' (364)

However, there is more to Martina than her civilized New York existence. Her full name, Martina *Twain*, echoes the pseudonym of an iconic American writer but also encrypts her metaphoric relationship with Self's new-found English literary acquaintance: she is a double, Martin A *bis*. Martin Amis the character is also a helper figure, though not a redeemer, more a specialist in literary rescue. Braving Self's initial, reflexive hostility to him as a cultural type, he accepts the commission to rewrite the script of *Good Money*, the film Self believes he is making in New York. However, in retrieving the possibility of an eventual production, Martin unwittingly assists in the collapse of the elaborate con and the ruin of its victim, Self. He loses his own fee, but, as he says, takes what he can, what Self never knew he had, namely, the secret of a scheme to humiliate and bankrupt someone like himself – or, in other words, a plot idea for Martin Amis, novelist.

The plot itself is little more than a pretext, and its relative probabilities are beside the point. *Money* is an unrelenting satire on the late twentieth century's culture of consumption, centred on the film and advertising industries and focused through their own Candide, the debauched innocent John Self. Debauched, and as such an extreme instance of the prevailing mass-hedonistic norm, yet innocent in his capacity to be fooled, Self is always the last to find out, and even then has difficulty in absorbing the revelation, and this does not change. His new girlfriend, the 'fat nurse' Georgina, represents the promise of care, not the hope of redemption. For him, history has reached an end-state:

> *You know, during that time of pills and booze, during that time of*
> *suicide, my entire future flashed through my head. And guess what. It*

was all a drag! My past at least was – what? It was … rich. And now
my life has lost its form. Now my life is only present, more present,
continuous present. (392, italics original)

Looking back on his last meeting with his London script
doctor, Self reports: 'When I awoke, Martin was gone and there
was no sound anywhere' (379). What the novelist has taken is
not only a plot idea but a voice and its speech repertoire. *Money*
is satire and its vector is style, the ironic low style to which the
novel takes pains to advert us. The idiolect that Amis creates
for his protagonist is in part textbook mid-Atlantic demotic,
freighted with the vocabulary of consumer brands and the culture
industry, in part an invented slang still more extravagant than
the Cockney it parodies; and embedded in its context of reference is all the high culture that Self has either forgotten or simply
does not know and cannot guess at. The cultural gulf internal to
this contrived language is Amis's contemplative substitute for a
power of critical leverage that he takes to have vanished from the
historical world. All that remains of culture as principle now is a
dandy's stratagem, for which the commanding English-language
precedent is Nabokov's *Lolita*, with its polystylist-protagonist,
Humbert Humbert. The dandy is a creature of sunset, as Baudelaire thought, and the parting gesture of Amis's exercise in style,
with its high-cultural simulation of low-or-no-cultural futility,
is to insist that art is not mocked, not even now, when virtually
everything has been lost.[3]

---

3 Charles Baudelaire, 'The Painter of Modern Life', in *The Painter of*
Modern Life and Other Essays, London and New York, 1995, p. 29.

2

> ... the cultures have mingled, and
> the forms have dissolved into chaos
>
> F.R. Leavis

Money is 'a suicide note'; *The Enigma of Arrival*, in contrast, narrates a process of rebirth and 'a second childhood of seeing and learning'.[4] The inter-communication of literature and landscape is equally strongly marked in the rural setting of this freely drawn memoir called 'a novel', whose anonymous narrator it would be pedantic to deny the name of the author, V.S. Naipaul. The sight of an old countryman at work suggests an unwritten poem by Wordsworth, 'The Fuel-Gatherer'; the sheep-shearing might be out of Hardy. A neighbour's garden is a Book of Hours, and his geese illuminate an obscure passage in *King Lear*. Other scenes recall the illustrations of *The Wind in the Willows*, or Constable, and the advance of autumn prompts a return to the winter journey in *Sir Gawain and the Green Knight*. The cardinal tropes of historical reflection – perdurance, continuity and its breaches, mutability, decay – are at the heart of these associations, and also of the novel's absorbed, circling micrological ruminations on a West of England landscape whose multi-millennial archaeology extends from Stonehenge to the high-tech debris of military exercises, including, now as its centrepiece, the manor house of a once-great estate near Salisbury.

---

4   V.S. Naipaul, *The Enigma of Arrival: A Novel in Five Sections*, London, 1987, p. 82. Further page references appear in brackets in the main text. (F.R. Leavis's words come from his Minority Press pamphlet *D.H. Lawrence* [1930], reprinted in *For Continuity*, Cambridge, 1933, p. 139.)

However, Naipaul's literary countryside is hardly a benign antithesis to Amis's neon-scorched city. The point of these associations and ruminations is that the inferences they prompt are likely to be mistaken, being framed by pre-given ways of looking, most significantly those of a colonial education, which must be worked through as a condition of seeing and learning to write. The value of culture depends on its continuing dialectical life. Thus, settled ways and settled people turn out to be novelties and newcomers. Changelessness is nothing of the kind. With 'so many ruins and restorations', with people possessed by 'the idea of being successors and inheritors' (50–1), historical narratives are not the self-evident accounts they can appear to be. The country is conventionally presented as a place of release from the complications of town living, but it happens in more than one case that neighbours find new, more sustaining social relationships through the reverse historical move, from tied cottages to urban housing estates. More portentously, the Edwardian manor in whose grounds the Naipaul-figure has come to live is well on its way to 'ruin', yet its gardens and water-meadows are full of unabating life, which captivates him. A survival from the glory days of the Empire, the manor offers an allegory of English 'decay', and in this there are relevant comparisons to be made with Forster and Waugh, but Naipaul resists 'that too ready idea of decay', just as he emphasizes that in the 'perfection' the estate once embodied 'there would have been no room for me', a Trinidadian of Indian descent – 'even now', in the 1970s and after, 'my presence was a little unlikely' (52). His solitary writer's life amidst the spreading wilderness of the manor is another kind of perfection, a confirmation of his childhood image of England and a balm for his chronically raw 'stranger's nerves', but no more likely to last, for the reality of history, he comes to believe, is flux and mutability, favouring an ethic of 'readiness for change, for living for what comes' (216).[5]

Ancient though such wisdom is, 'possibly ancestral' as the Naipaul-figure notes, recalling his Hindu forebears, its animating conditions are fully contemporary. The idea of flux is a stoic defence against the flux itself, of which, he makes clear, he is himself an emblematic case. Arriving in London from the Caribbean some twenty-five years previously, around 1950, he 'had found [himself] at the beginning of a great movement of peoples after the war, a great shaking up of the world, a great shaking up of old cultures and old ideas' (145). This was not the London foreknown from Dickens, nor was it any longer the locus of imperial magic, which 'belonged to the past' (120). Here was the beginning of another kind of end-state, what he soon came to think of as the ontological 'disorder' of modern postcoloniality.

The Enigma of Arrival and *The Mimic Men* are companion pieces, the more strikingly so for the twenty years that separate them. The earlier of the two narrates the life of an Indo-Caribbean man, Ralph Kripalsingh, to the age of forty; the later one unfolds in the middle age of a Naipaul-like writer and looks back on a Trinidadian boyhood from his retreat in the Wiltshire countryside. Personal narratives both, they move easily between storytelling and reflection of a more or less general cast, in a form that suggests its own distinct category, the novel as essay. While *The Enigma of Arrival* cultivates a prose of brooding repetition, *The Mimic Men* leans to aphorism, at times approaching satire, and

---

5   Grammar modified for context.

is centred on a passage of social and public engagement, unlike its companion, which is devoted to a place of retreat and repair.

The substance of *The Mimic Men* is a clearly delineated historical situation: the last decades of British rule in the fictional Caribbean island of Isabella seen through the eyes of a boy stirred by romantic images of a high Indic patrimony and framed overall by the culture of a colonial grammar school.[6] Indeed, conceived and written as it was in a decade that saw the United Nations increase its membership by more than half, largely as a consequence of the great post-war wave of decolonization in Asia, Africa and the Caribbean, the novel was a topical intervention of a kind.[7] Its message – for once the word is not reductive – was plain, emphatic and desolate. The end of the colonial era did not signify the transition from an oppressive imperial order to another one founded on independence and equality at home and in the world, as liberationist political programmes had envisioned. Its meaning was the advent of a general 'disorder' without limit of time, in which political frustration and failure were conspicuous and damaging yet, finally, just a symptom of an endemic cultural condition, another dystopian end-state. The

---

6   V.S. Naipaul, *The Mimic Men* (1967), London, 1969, p. 32. Further page references appear in brackets in the main text.

7   Founded in 1945 with fifty-one member-states, the UN numbered seventy-six after a decade, and by 1965 had gained a further forty-one, making a total of 117 and a ten-year increase of more than half. One year alone, 1960, saw the arrival of seventeen new African states. Trinidad and Tobago, along with Jamaica, joined in 1962. The composition of *The Mimic Men* is dated August 1964–July 1966. It was substantially written during a university residency in Kampala in the first half of 1966, some four years after Ugandan independence. See Patrick French, *The World Is What It Is: The Authorized Biography of V.S. Naipaul*, London, 2008.

story of Isabella's path to independence and early experience of self-rule is easily recognized and classified. The improvisations and incoherencies of strategy and programme in the anti-colonial movement; the discovery of the effective limits of sovereignty, as metropolitan big business exploits its inbuilt advantages and the former imperial power, faced with a threat to historic economic interests, makes plain the limits of its indulgence; the violent deterioration in inter-communal relations as a displaced popular response to general political blockage; the character of the new ruling elite, aspirational, shallow and quick to settle for the trappings and the pickings of office, comforts in the face of the likely fall: these have been recurring elements in the history of the semi- or neo-colonial world, though none is peculiar to it. But even that designation can appear pretentious, as also might the claim that the record can be called a 'history'.

Ralph, at forty years of age a political exile in London, has thought of writing, if not such a history then at least a sketch for it – 'there is no such thing as history nowadays; there are only manifestos and antiquarian research; and on the subject of empire there is only the pamphleteering of churls' (32). What he writes in the event – his text is the entire substance of Naipaul's novel – is closer to autobiography than memoir in form, as if confirming that his public life and the collective action he was a part of make no larger sense.

> They talk of the pace of postwar political change. It is not the pace of creation. Nor is it the pace of destruction, as some think. Both these things require time. The pace of events, as I see it, is no more than the pace of chaos on which strict limits have been imposed. (192)

It is an acute phase in a disorder that has the depth and persistence of an ontological state: 'The empires of our time were short-lived, but they have altered the world for ever; their passing away is their least significant feature.' The psycho-cultural damage they did is irreparable:

> It was my hope [in writing, Ralph records,] to give expression to the restlessness, the deep disorder, which the great explorations, the overthrow in three continents of established social organizations, the unnatural bringing together of peoples who could achieve fulfilment only within the security of their own societies and the landscapes hymned by their ancestors, it was my hope to give partial expression to the restlessness which this great upheaval has brought about. (32)

The restlessness is the consequence of a radical alienation and dislocation; its aesthetic, the contrary of Herder's spontaneous image of happiness, is mimicry. The simulation is perhaps most evident when it is projected in public: Isabella's new rulers travel in official cars bearing the initial *M* – M for minister and also for mimicry. But it is active in everything. Ralph has an indelible memory of giving his teacher an apple, a fruit unknown in Isabella but nevertheless mandatory in this staple convention of English school stories. Alienation speaks ironically in the grammar of his very first sentence: 'When I first came to London, shortly after the end of the war, *I found myself* after a few days in a boarding-house, called a private hotel, in the Kensington High Street area' (5, my italics). How far from simply reflexive the sense of that verb turns out to be is already indicated in his misnamed lodgings, and in his room, which contains not one mirror but many, as if to authenticate more than one version of its occupant. The misnomer is also the first sign that London, the 'famous', the 'magical' city, is not quite itself. The landlord is out of English literature, yet not *echt* English: his name is Shylock. His house is a way-station in 'the great movement of peoples' that Naipaul looked back on twenty years later in *The Enigma of Arrival*, a temporary home to Kenyan, Maltese, Italian, Burmese; a Moroccan French translator of American thrillers, a Jew of no national designation and a solitary Cockney. In this motley gathering, Ralph finds a self to mimic – the 'character' of 'the dandy, the extravagant colonial' neglectful of his studies – but not 'the god of the city' he has looked to, 'the great city, centre of the world, in which, fleeing disorder, I had hoped to find the beginning of order' (20, 18). Fleeing a second time, as a defeated politician, he sees the great city as 'the greater disorder, the final emptiness: London and the home counties' (8).

The disorder is general, not sparing the old imperial capital, the presumptive locus of truth and order, even if in delivering this final judgement on the city, Ralph continues to honour its customary authority in his sense of things. His adult life in Isabella, the time of his business (successful) and marriage (unsuccessful), then his rise and fall in politics, was 'a parenthesis', he concludes; however, the form of his autobiography suggests a still more drastic evaluation. The order of his life-history shows an alternation of place between Isabella and London: he was born and schooled in Isabella, went to university in London, returned to Isabella for some twenty years, and is now back in London in exile. But the order of narration reworks this real sequence, opening with his student days, continuing with the first stage of his adult life in Isabella, moving back then to his youth before recounting his political career on the island, and closing with his new life in London and the composition of *The Mimic Men*. The locative sequence now runs London – Isabella – London. Or, in the terms of the metaphor at hand, it is not just the prime years of adulthood that are in parenthesis, but Isabella itself. The story of Ralph's life so far begins and ends in London, the great metropolis of his youth, from where Isabella is framed and seen, 'an obscure New World transplantation, second-hand and barbarous' (118). And yet life so measured has been a progress from a boarding-house to a private hotel, from temporary to unending transience. The idea of London has made a nonsense of the idea of Isabella but is itself now a void. Even the comfort of his regressive sexuality, with its fixation on the female breast, is taken away: the shapely but self-absorbed Sandra, the trophy bride from his student days, has left him, and Lady Stella Stockwell, who feeds him English nursery stories in the midst of his final political humiliation in London, has no breasts to speak of (231). Nothing remains at last but the shards of his classical education – tokens of cultural order, to which he turns, as if ritually, in moments of strong feeling – and writing, which, 'for all its initial distortion, clarifies, and even becomes a process of life' (251).[8]

---

8 *Dixi*, Ralph declares, 'I have spoken', and who will query his last word? The experience seems definitive. But a more telling envoi would have been *rescripsi* – for objectively, and perhaps in some way intentionally, *The Mimic Men* sets its face against another appraisal of postcolonial prospects, in effect rewriting a novel published just three years earlier, under the same imprint, Waguih Ghali's *Beer in the Snooker Club*. Ghali's protagonist, Ram, is an Egyptian Copt in his twenties at the time of the Suez crisis, alienated equally from his wealthy landowning family and from the repressive state that is taking shape after Nasser's revolution. His Anglophile education has

A companion piece to this novel, *The Enigma of Arrival* is also a
continuation of it, in part because of the biographical-historical
sequences and situations that recur in different workings, but
more significantly for its marked intensification of the thematic
commitments of its predecessor. Here the etched vision of post-
war London is followed by the slow, painstaking composition of
a country landscape and its real or inferred histories, in which
Naipaul becomes a kind of micro-ethnographer, absorbed in his
fellow 'campers in the ruins', his neighbours in a historically res-
onant stretch of post-imperial England. Self-examination is again
a central theme, though this time the existential stakes approach
the marvellous, as the narrator finds a redeemed 'second life', 'a
second, happier childhood' (82–3).

---

drawn him to the northern ice, to London, with its red buses and draught ale,
and the *New Statesman* – and so to a personal condition he quickly comes to
understand as self-alienated mimicry. He is, he says, an Egyptian – an affirmation his Jewish communist lover would challenge – but cannot say what
that might mean. The prospect with which the novel ends settles nothing: a
marriage to a beautiful, politically conformist woman of his own class that
may or may not succeed. It is an anti-climactic pause, lacking finality, and in
this, past all the arresting similarities, lies one fundamental difference from
the counter-narrative that Naipaul would publish a few years later. The other
lies in the ternary narrative scheme that both novels adopt. Naipaul's locative
order, London – Isabella – London, is the reverse of Ghali's, in which the
London adventure is an inset in a story of Cairo. Thus, his novel suggests,
however discouraging and even absurd the situation may be, Egypt remains
the ground on which the future will be made. Written in English by a communist in exile, begun in Stockholm, completed in Germany and published
in Britain (by André Deutsch), *Beer in the Snooker Club* is a work of critical
cosmopolitanism quite free of the historical nihilism that drives *The Mimic
Men*. (Ghali's novel deserves fuller, more integrated treatment than I have
been able to give it here. I came upon it only when this book was already more
or less done.)

Above all, the narrator of *Enigma of Arrival* embodies a further rarefaction of Ralph's eventual commitment to writing as an ethic of existence. In this case, the vocation is an old one, not a mid-life discovery. But its fulfilment requires rebirth, an ascetic emptying out and renewal of perception, in domestic solitude. The sheer abstraction of the commitment to 'writing' is telling. It suggests a vestigial cultural practice, little more than the mark of an idea of true judgement in overwhelmingly adverse conditions. These novels narrate a circular movement, each closing with the discovery of the image that frees the protagonist to write it, and in this they stand alongside *Money*, another novel in which a solitary writer makes art out of a catastrophe, as fictions of literary autogenesis. They are, as a group, disinherited offspring of *Orlando*, all of them nihilistic in their different ways – examples of what culture is reduced to, once its enabling conditions have disintegrated.

3

Is it your culture? Is it culture at all?

The Black Album

Shahid Hasan is another writer of sub-continental background, the son of settled, prosperous Pakistani immigrants in the travel business in suburban Kent. Hanif Kureishi's *The Black Album*, whose protagonist he is, tells the story of his *Bildung*. If a fiction like *The Mimic Men* can reasonably be described as 'philosophical' by virtue of the generality of its postulates, Kureishi's novel belongs unmistakably in that category: it is a novel of ideas dramatizing a discussion whose crux is the disputed nature of the good life, or culture.

It is 1989. Shahid has come to London after his father's death, with 'a bunch of Prince records, and a ton of books', to study and to take a reflective distance from his family and its history. The crises and contentions of the time are alive in his run-down college – which is itself an exhibit, now functioning in effect as an organized pastime for unemployed youth. The disintegration of the European Communist bloc is audible in the deteriorating stammer of a Marxist history lecturer, Brownlow; contemporary popular culture is the unorthodox forte of his liberal studies tutor, Deedee Osgood, whose reputation has drawn him there in the first place; the controversy over Salman Rushdie's novel *The Satanic Verses* is in full spate, and in the student body, the ascetic Islamo-populist Riaz and his followers are determined to avenge this affront to customary belief.

The culture of Shahid's parents is philistine, and self-deluding about racism, which in different ways – the father too much the Anglophile, his wife too genteel – they have wished away. Brother Chili, also in the travel business, is a bundle of appetites, flash, with a taste for the high life and complete scorn for 'losers'. However, Shahid has inherited a love of reading indirectly, from his journalist uncle Asif, who has resettled in Pakistan but left behind his library, a freethinker's medley of 'Joad, Laski and Popper, and studies of Freud, along with Maupassant, Henry Miller and the Russians'.[9] He goes on reading hungrily, Proust beside Kafka, Faulkner and Morrison, and writing. As his commitment to high literary culture develops and hardens, he becomes increasingly removed from his peers, 'few of whom

---

9   Hanif Kureishi, *The Black Album*, London, 1995, p. 16. Further page references appear in brackets in the main text.

even had books in their houses ... only gardening guides, atlases, Readers Digests' (22). So now he has come to London, eager for understanding, alone for the first time in a multi-ethnic student hostel, and off balance.

He soon finds the 'new people' he is looking for, and a new cultural antithesis to organize and disorganize his life. In Deedee Osgood, with her novel conjugations of American popular culture and the politics of race, he finds the intellectual stimulus he craves, even if he wonders about the 'post-modern ... freedom of instruction' she offers, and her sceptical attitude to high culture and the 'migraine reads' to which he remains committed. The final emphasis in her personal culture is hedonistic – she loves music and dance, wine, drugs and sex, all of which she shares with Shahid in due course. 'Is life just for pleasure, then?' he asks in a tense moment. 'What else is there?' she replies (91). Libertarian hedonism is her credo and her temporal perspective is set accordingly. When Shahid answers her proposal that

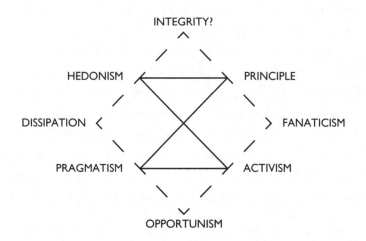

Figure 4 *The Black Album*

he wear make-up with a hesitant 'Now?', she replies 'There's only now' (97). For Riaz, in polar contrast, the 'one thing' that matters is 'the future and how to forge it' (124). Legal adviser to poor fellow-Muslims and scourge of Western spiritual nullity, Riaz is a man of principle. Shahid's family 'have lost themselves', he quickly decides, and Chili is a 'dissipator' (6). Shahid, on the other hand, appears to be 'searching for something', and Riaz knows what it is: 'the very biggest thing of all', unconditional fidelity to religious and ethnic origins. For much of the narrative, Shahid will vacillate between these competing poles of attraction, increasingly drawn by the intellectual and sensuous pleasures of his times with Deedee but drawn also by the idea of community to which Riaz and his 'brothers and sisters', for all their obscurantism, bear practical witness in their readiness to take direct action against racism.

Racism defines the political foreground of *The Black Album*, which is, among other things, a study in the generational dynamics of Islamism in Britain.[10] There is another historical context, however, which comes into view once the semantic design of the narrative is taken as a whole (Figure 4). *Hedonism* and *principle*, represented by Deedee and Riaz respectively, are the leading contraries; their respective contradictories are *activism* and *pragmatism*, which thus oppose one another as sub-contraries. This is the map of what is possible and what is ruled out, and two features of it deserve particular comment. The first is that these four structuring values (and their cognates), which in the narrative present appear as a field of tensions rising from serious to

---

10   A better-known instance is Kureishi's story 'My Son the Fanatic', which was first published in *The New Yorker* in 1994, a year before *The Black Album*, and later adapted as the film of the same title (1997).

absolute, are re-narrated in a momentary recollection as having once formed a spontaneous unity. Here is Deedee, who has been telling Shahid about her political past and how she came to marry Brownlow:

> 'From the middle of the 1970s there was always the Party. If I wasn't studying, I was at meetings, or selling papers or standing on the picket line. I met Brownlow.'
> 'What did you see in him?'
> 'We liked the Beatles. We had activism and talk in common. We imagined we were on the Left Bank, running into our lovers in cafés, living without bourgeois jealousy, committed to personal and political change. Sartre and De Beauvoir have much to be responsible for.' (95)

Principle, pleasure and activism communicate fluently in this scene, and the implicit judgement of unrealism is both relative and retrospective. Thus, there remains, implicit in the semantics of the novel, a background contrast between then and now, between the '70s and the late '80s, a framing narrative of a once energetic and hopeful left now defeated and beyond recovery. Brownlow, drunk and now jobless, sums up for Shahid:

> '… everything I believed has turned into shit. There we were, right up to the end of the seventies, arguing about society after the r-revolution, the nature of the dialectic, the meaning of history. And all the while, as we debated in our journals, it was being taken from us. The British people didn't want e-education, housing, the a-arts, justice, equality…'
> 'Why's that?'

'Because they're a bunch of fucking greedy, myopic c-cunts.'

'The working class?'

'Yes! … I can't say they've betrayed us – though I think it, I do! It's not true, not true! They've betrayed themselves!' (202)

Kureishi's near-future vision of social devastation in East London and the gallery of drug-blasted grotesques who haunt the Morlock pub extends and varies Brownlow's portrayal without displacing it. This is London after the passing of social hope, and in the semantic scheme of *The Black Album* the narrative vertices indicate the remaining possibilities. The resolution of principle and activism, to the right of the square, is now the privilege of Islamist fanatics; Brownlow has become a ridiculous caricature of himself, so addled by his years of militancy that he supports the public burning of Rushdie's novel. The union of hedonism and pragmatism, to the left, yields only Chili, 'the Reality Guide' whose decade the '80s have been: a Thatcherite, his brother says, and 'a lesson in how not to live' (207). The resolution of pragmatism and activism is embodied in another political grotesque, the opportunist Labour councillor George Rugman Rudder. The remaining option, a resolution of principle and hedonism, is embodied in the figure of Asif, the whisky-drinking radical journalist who has done time in a Pakistani jail for his resistance to the Islamizing policies of the Zia regime. But he is, precisely, absent. There remains only Shahid.

The second notable feature of the narrative semantics of the novel is that Shahid remains unsettled within the design. His possible fates are those of his own cultural principle, which asserts the cardinal value of freedom in writing and reading. This is the stake in the twin crises of his relations with Riaz, both of them literary. Timid at first in his misgivings about the plan to burn *The Satanic Verses*, Shahid breaks ranks just as the flame is lit. In a complementary act of dissent, he creatively reprogrammes the solemn task of transcribing Riaz's pious verses to computer, interweaving erotic compositions of his own. Both acts align him with Deedee, and thus suggest the possibility of an available resolution of the tension between principle and hedonism. As the finale of the novel opens, Shahid, having risen early, returns to Deedee's bedroom, not to wake her but to begin to write 'with concentrated excitement. He had to find some sense in his recent experiences; he wanted to know and understand. ... He would spread himself out, in his work and in love, following his curiosity' (228). It is a moment of respite in a dark, mordant narrative, but it is not a resolution. If the work he has begun to write should turn out, in the familiar trope of autogenesis, to be something like *The Black Album*, then his project of self-discovery will have ended in paradox. In the closing sequence of the novel, the lovers go away for a weekend at the seaside, and there they agree they will stay together 'until it stops being fun' (230). Their compact, which is the only proffered security for writing and culture, could hardly be more abstract or precarious. Shahid, having begun his search in a dingy rented room, has come to temporary rest in a cheap bed-and-breakfast. The prospectus for the 'new adventure' is notably one-sided: escape from the everyday, indefinitely prolonged time out, a Prince concert, and, after all the cultural agonistics, the bathos of 'fun'. Deedee has planned it all – 'He didn't have to think about anything.'

4

Amis, Naipaul and Kureishi all recount the approach to a cultural end-state under the pressure of overwhelming historical forces: consumer capitalism; colonialism and its sequels; or both, the reverse migrations of the postcolonial era being textured now by the neo-liberal ascendancy in the world economy and the defeat of the left in all its principal varieties. Satire is more or less pronounced in all three cases and the surviving warrant of cultural value is the figure of the writer, who is isolated or only temporarily attached. Zadie Smith's *On Beauty*, in contrast, returns in explicit homage to the complex comedy of *Howards End*, affirming the sovereign moral power of conviviality.

Indeed, the transfers of diegetic material – situations and events – from Forster's novel to Smith's are so extensive and conspicuous that it seems apt to speak of the later work as paralleling the earlier one. *On Beauty* begins by rewriting the opening sentence of *Howards End* – 'One may as well begin with Jerome's e-mails to his father'[11] – and develops into a variation on its first chapter as a whole. But rather more than differences of sex, biological relationship and means of communication separate Jerome Belsey and his father, Howard, from the Schlegel sisters. The Helen-figure is someone else (his sister, Zora), and Howard, in polar contrast with Margaret, will soon emerge as a negative value in the narrative design. So will Sir Monty, the head of the Kipps household, where Jerome, an accidental guest, has fallen in love with the beautiful daughter, Victoria. But for now the two men, who are both academics, stand in opposite corners, having

---

11   Zadie Smith, *On Beauty* (2005), London, 2006, p. 3. Further page references appear in brackets in the main text.

clashed publicly over Rembrandt, to whom Monty has devoted one of his numerous books and whose iconic cultural standing is the critical target of the monograph that Howard has been writing for most of his career. Howard's intellectual mission is the battle against humanism, in the severe post-structuralist manner of the 1980s, to which Monty is haughtily opposed on traditionalist grounds: Rembrandt is a great artist, above all – but art appreciation is forbidden in the Belsey classroom. These scholarly differences are embedded in a wider cultural politics. Howard, a white Londoner who has married and had children with a black American, Kiki, is a liberal in the US sense, leading the drive for affirmative action at Wellington, the New England college where he teaches. Monty, a black Trinidadian settled in London with his Afro-Caribbean wife and their English-born children, is a Christian and a cultural conservative who believes that such measures are fraudulent. And now he has turned up in Howard's college as visiting faculty, intent on challenging the liberal ascendancy in the 'liberal arts'.

Here is the substance of a novel of ideas to set beside *The Black Album* as a transatlantic counterpart, even if Smith's protagonists are mainly Londoners. Within a shared liberal political frame-work, the Belsey household presents a gallery of varieties. Zora, now a sophomore at Wellington, identifies with her father and reproduces his intellectual manner, at higher speed and volume. Jerome, in contrast, has become a Christian and is concerned that his secular family should acknowledge his choice. Kiki, a veteran of 'womanish' struggles over race and gender, is disturbed by her husband's strict, unbending demonstrations of principle, which extend to a domestic ban on hanging figurative art. Levi, the youngest child and the only one born in the USA, is culturally post-literate: his medium is music and his desire is to merge into the culture of black Boston, the antitype of his quiet college-town suburb. The Kippses are on the face of it less differentiated, for a reason that inheres in their cultural coding. The Belsey domestic narrative is like an ensemble piece, the characters in permanent interaction, never far from tumult: it is a hyperbolic sign of freedom. The Kipps household, by contrast, is a model of peaceful order directed by Monty's principles and sustained, as Jerome reports, by his wife's 'angelic' ministrations. However, this ideal division of labour, with the politico-cultural contrast it upholds, is before long transfigured into a pattern of contrariety: one of a more abstract kind that constitutes the central dialectic of the novel.

Kiki Belsey, refusing to be controlled by the logic of her husband's academic feud, pays a welcoming visit to her new neighbour, Carlene Kipps. The two women strike up an immediate rapport, and the conversation flows quickly, soon reaching the turn where Carlene says:

'I love a line from a poem: *There is such a shelter in each other.* I think it is so *fine*. Don't you think it's a wonderful thing?' ...

'Is it – which poet is it?'

'Oh, I would not actually know that for myself ... Monty is the intellectual in our family. I have no talent for ideas or memory for names. I read it in a newspaper, that's all. You're an intellectual too?'

And this was possibly the most important question Wellington had never honestly asked Kiki.

'No, actually ... No, I'm not. I'm really not.'

'Neither am I.' (93–4)

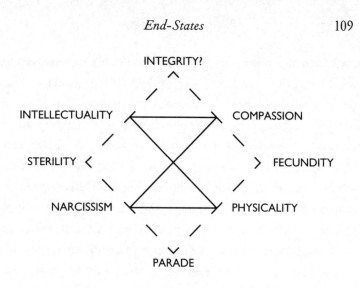

Figure 5 *On Beauty*

This is a defining exchange. Not-an-intellectual is an identity now claimed by three characters (the first in time is Carlene's son, Michael) and one of the most positive the fiction can bestow, in its association with a cluster of other positives including love, instinct, forgiveness, shelter and (one word to do service for them all) compassion. *Compassion* names one pole of the novel's narrative semantics in its resistance to its opposite, the ruling value of *intellectuality* (Figure 5). Dogmatism and censoriousness are natural specialized outgrowths of this value, but it is the generality of lives governed by intellect that is pilloried in the novel, which continues the ancient Menippean tradition of mocking learned men. 'Men' is an exclusive universal here: the 'intellectuals' of the novel are female as well as male and are similarly deformed or stunted. Zora 'lives through footnotes', thinks Kiki (70); in contrast with her classmates, who continue to 'like' things, she might be 'a text-eating *machine*', Howard's teaching assistant reports approvingly, a destroyer who 'strips' and 'rips apart' whatever literature comes her way (149). Claire Malcolm, a colleague and sometime lover of Howard's, is a poet and thus presumptively exempt from such tendencies, but Kiki has noticed 'the implacable intelligence of her eyes', which, when she laughs, do not 'indulge in the natural release of the act' (52). Nevertheless, it is men who set the tone, and women – mothers, to be exact – who nurture all that is good and necessary in being not-an-intellectual. Carlene's decision to bequeath a precious painting to Kiki, rather than let it pass into Monty's valuable collection of Haitian art, is the token of this in the narrative present of the novel. Beyond it, and in keeping, is the closing suggestion that Kiki's decision to leave Howard may not be quite irrevocable – that the Belsey house, which is in fact her own by inheritance, may again shelter all the family. And in Levi, who has no use for universities and hardly more for books but nevertheless comes to qualify his allegiance to the 'street' in refusing the abusive elements of its sexual culture, the novel intimates another aspect of a desirable future, for which the novel's term is simply 'human'.

Diagonally opposite *compassion*, as its contradictory, is *narcissism*. It is the unity of intellectualism with this subjective disposition that defines Howard and Monty, who are both self-absorbed to the point of moral dysfunction. Both family histories have been dominated by their respective intellectual manias. Howard prefers his people served 'in a nutshell'; his unsteady sense of the independent reality of others is a commonplace in his household, and is quickly perceived by new acquaintances such as Victoria Kipps (or Vee), whom he toys with, and humiliates both socially and sexually. In Monty, narcissism steps forth as impersonal rectitude set off by simple male vanity. He is a textbook paterfamilias and his transgressions are styled accordingly:

an old-fashioned hypocrite, he publicly deplores the presence of 'discretionary' young blacks in classes for which they are formally unqualified but seduces one of them (Chantelle) anyway, later banishing her when she becomes an inconvenience.

Only two of the men in Smith's novel seem at all equipped to redeem the condition of 'intellectual' from the disrepute in which it lies. One is Jerome, who combines his father's academic capabilities with his mother's power of empathy and thus seems in principle well placed to resolve the tension between intellectualism and compassion. Yet his narrative ends inconclusively. His elective Christianity signifies independence of a kind but also, so far as the novel shows, entails marginality. The other is Carl, a poet and the most significant of the discretionaries. Meeting the Belseys at an outdoor Mozart recital, in a moment of confusion over portable music players, he makes a lasting impression on Zora with his arresting good looks, and is later talent-spotted by Claire Malcolm, who invites him to join her Creative Writing class. Carl is the Bast-figure in the novel, a young man 'trying to get a stage higher with [his] life' (418) and apparently lucky in his chance encounters. He flourishes, becoming a music archivist in Wellington's Black Studies Department and taking up with Vee, but with disastrous consequences. In an altercation with a drunk and jealous Zora, he reveals what Chantelle, his neighbour, has told him about Monty, and hints that there is more in the same vein to say about Howard. The evidence, in his eyes, damns the entire cultural caste he has been gratified to come near to. Zora gives him his opening when she defends her father and his colleagues as '*grown-ups*. They're *intellectuals* – not children. They don't act like hound-dog teenagers every time some cute piece of ass comes shimmying up to them' (418). Carl responds with a final judgement: 'You need to hear some truth. All of you people, you *intellectuals* ... You got your college degrees, but you don't even live right. You people are all the same ... I need to be with *my people*, man – I can't do this no more' (418–9). And with that he leaves Wellington and Zora, whose subsequent efforts to trace him come to nothing. The cultural possibility that he embodied has been rescinded.

Vee leaves too, but in a strikingly different mode. Whereas Carl's disappearance is an event within the fiction, with a reported aftermath, Vee simply walks through a door, 'distraught' and 'broken', and is never seen or heard of again. She exits like an actor passing from the intelligible world of the play-space into the unscripted void backstage. It is as though she has been cancelled. What leaves with her? In the first place, a certain received idea of beauty. Vee, like Carl, is tall, slender and extravagantly good-looking, an epitome of golden youth, forming a polar contrast with Kiki, whose middle-aged obesity is equally marked. Furthermore, she is extravagantly sexual, compelling to all the men she encounters and, to those she favours, such as Howard and Carl, gratifyingly active and uninhibited – her repertoire, like Selina's in *Money*, including a line in auto-pornography. Vee is the perfectly desirable body, and in this reductive sense the ultimate in narcissistic non-intellectual being. She exits like an actor because that has been her mode throughout. Her seemingly limitless wardrobe and styling are a performance resource, accessories for the continuous parade of herself. That she is intelligent and has some critical understanding of her masquerade is true enough. [12] But her presence and force in the symbolic design of

_____

12 This understanding remains semi-obscure. See her confronting Howard, after their final miscarried assignation in a Boston hotel (390).

the narrative are those of a sexualized body. If this were *Howards End*, she would be Jacky.

Vee would be Jacky, and Howard would be Tibby. *On Beauty* varies its Forsterian model most drastically by promoting these minor characters to central roles, but – crucially – does so without moderating their symbolic extremism. Thus it remains, here as in the original, that they cannot be contained as they are, in any of the available narrative resolutions. Vee must go, and Howard, if he is ever to be forgiven, must be broken – must become an intellectual Henry Wilcox. This is the work of the closing episode, in which Howard is to give his long-awaited public lecture on Rembrandt. He arrives late and flustered and, as he then discovers, without his notes. Lacking these written words, he cannot speak; he and his audience are left alone with the projected images, which now command the occasion. ' "*Hendrickje Bathing*, 1654", croaked Howard and said no more' (442). The audience, including friends and acolytes from Wellington, is 'perplexed', but Howard has spotted Kiki. He enlarges the image so that 'the woman's fleshiness filled the wall' (443). He smiles at his wife, who smiles too, if not quite in return. The remaining sentences of the novel, narrated from Howard's point of view, simply render the painting of Hendrickje's skin tone and the meanings it suggests – a utopian promise or a sobering reminder of ageing or both, since love and hope are no longer the monopoly of stereotypical youth: 'chalky whites and lively pinks, the underlying blue of her veins and the ever present human hint of yellow, intimation of what is to come' (442). Silent, wordless, simply looking at last, Howard has been released from the prison of intellect.

*   *   *

Resistance to intellectualism, however sympathetic its motives may be, must always run the risk of anti-intellectualism pure and simple, as it certainly does in *On Beauty*, where the pursuit of the academic named Belsey is unrelenting from the start,[13] and where, in the absence of an adequate counter-instance, the vocation of intellectual seems compromised beyond repair. 'We murder to dissect' is the unwritten Wordsworthian motto of the novel.[14] There is some irony in this, since the unfolding of the narrative brings a parallel disclosure of the limits of the alter-ethos, compassion.

In a subplot for which the term itself might well have been invented, the micro-society of Wellington academia is shown to rest on cheap migrant labour from Haiti. The beneficiaries of this underworld of domestics and other menials, taxi-drivers and hustlers selling fake accessories on the streets, are in the first place the members of a bourgeoisie, a class rather than a racial group, even if its membership is disproportionately white. The distinguished academic who amasses a fortune in popular artworks from the island is a Caribbean black: Monty. Kiki is stunned to be told by her son, Levi, that she is sweating their household cleaner, Monique. Choo, who has been a high-school literature teacher at home, is abruptly declassed in his new setting, paid a pittance to serve wine to 'the big white professors' – including Monty as well as Howard. Contact between Haitian migrants and the Belseys is normal, therefore, and, in Levi's case, pursued in a developing spirit of solidarity, yet without any tangible narrative yield. Choo may be an intellectual among his people, but, as the

---

13   And, in reality, perhaps, *ad hominem* as well.

14   William Wordsworth, 'The Tables Turned', from *Lyrical Ballads* (1798).

probabilities stand, he has an even smaller chance than Jerome or Carl of renewing the moral authority that Howard and Monty have dissipated. He and his fellow-Haitians live beyond the uncross-able social boundary of the fiction, in an 'abyss' at least as deep as Forster's, and as in *Howards End* their narrative appearances can only be short-lived, since there are no available resolutions that embrace them. 'We are not concerned with the very poor', says Forster's narrator. 'They are unthinkable …'.[15] And: 'You know what, Levi?' Kiki says, 'her voice breaking', when her son makes his challenge. 'I don't want to talk to you anymore.' — ''Cause you ain't got no answer to that!' is his retort (429–30).

Kiki's eventual answer will be to sell the painting Carlene Kipps has left her and donate the proceeds to the Haitian Support Group — or so Levi informs his brother and sister, contradict-ing their own spontaneous guesswork. There is nothing more to confirm or correct his claim, since Haiti disappears from the narrative at just this point. Compassion finds a way, it seems, but only thanks to a double mediation: Forsterian 'connection', which is normatively personal, is here expressed as political support, which in turn takes the form of financial subsidy — and that, like Helen Schlegel's offer to Bast, can always be declined. There is nothing of Forster's symbolically rich resolution-effect in Kiki's gesture, and not a great deal more in the main finale, which leaves so much open. Intellectualism has been humbled as a cultural principle (Howard's end: the name is hardly an acci-dent). But what might be a better alternative, and who, if anyone, might vindicate it, Smith's novel does not tell us. It is all very far from a hayfield in England.

---

15   E.M. Forster, *Howards End*, p. 41.

The Condition of Culture Novel

It is tempting, in summing up a study of this kind, to bolt for closure, to strain the evidences of pattern and repetition in a well-made historical plot. I try to resist this in what follows now – which is not so much a synoptic 'conclusion' as a set of elaborations developing, each into the next, by a logic of association. Within these, and the restricted corpus of novels they concern, I generalize and interpret as far and as firmly as seems defensible, and, since modesty of intent is a limitation but not an excuse, with the usual intellectual obligations under the rules of coherence and respect of evidence. That said, we can turn to the English condition of culture novel, a genre indeed, with its characteristic narrative forms and topics, and a discernible historical meaning – the narrative of itself, which, while remaining open to the future, appears to have reached a significant pause and point of displacement around the end of the twentieth century, one hundred years or so after its emergence.

I

There are narratives of *situation* and narratives of *transformation*. This is one of the most basic distinctions to be made in the great trans-historical corpus of storytelling, inescapable whatever terminology is preferred, with whatever embedded assumptions and implications.[1] In the first kind of narrative, a given state of affairs prevails from start to finish, and its action, however full of incident, is essentially one of progressive illustration, elaboration or disclosure. In the other kind, there is an event, something occurring to produce a significant change, the transformation of the opening situation *a* into a new situation *b*. The contrast is one of proportion, not essence. The very idea of transformation presupposes a given situation and an imaginable alternative; and a narrative of situation without any incident betokening the possibility of change would be a contradiction in terms, a description lying across the boundary at which storytelling ceases.[2] All narratives are mixed, then, but the distinction remains fundamentally important. What might it tell us about the condition of culture novel?

Money is a simple instance of the narrative of situation, one

1 For Yuri Lotman, from whom I derive this basic suggestion, the opposite of *transformation* is at different times *classification* or *identity* or *cyclicality*, each choice suggesting a different emphasis in the narratives in question or a different thematic priority in analysis. (See Lotman, *The Universe of the Mind: A Semiotic Theory of Culture*, London, 1990, and *The Structure of the Artistic Text*, Ann Arbor, 1977.) The advantage of the term *situation* as an alternative option is simply its semantic range, which accommodates a variety of relevant inflections, personal, social-spatial and temporal.

2 If indeed it ever quite ceases, leaving pure description without narrative elements or functions: see Gérard Genette, 'Frontières du récit', *Figures II*, Paris, 1969, pp. 58–9.

in which the law is given by cupidity and its meretricious post-culture, which no one can resist successfully. Most of what happens in the novel is in this sense a non-event, just another predictable or allowable move within a closed and deadly game. *Orlando* is in one obvious respect an exemplar of the other kind of narrative: a spontaneous sex change is as radical a personal transformation as any. However, if Orlando's metamorphosis is in truth one of the main modalities of her self-perfection as the aristocrat he always was, then Woolf's novel appears differently, as a narrative of situation – which its depressive counterpart, *Between the Acts*, unmistakably is.[3]

Howards End, on the other hand, really is a narrative of trans-formation, though even here there are serious qualifications to enter. The closing situation of the novel is more secure and more settled than that of its opening: philistinism and advanced opinion have been moderated and both have come to rest in the country-side. However, this solution is plainly regressive – the shaping spirits at Howards End are a dead mother and an infant – and does not nullify the catastrophe on which it depends: the defeat of the novel's formative projects of transformation, namely Bast's struggle for self-education and Helen's will to release someone from poverty. In these ways, Forster typifies two strong tendencies in the condition of culture novel. Transformations are inessential in this genre, and where they are attempted they either entail a more or less radical social withdrawal – 'escape' would be the plainer word – or they fail. The new family at

---

3   It would take more than an adulterous liaison to offset the conditions of a marriage whose emotional violence is inscribed in the historical 'scars' of centuries and the blind impulses of nature – epitomized in the snake that chokes on the frog it tries to eat.

Howards End is a study in pastoral; the finale of *The Black Album* is a late-twentieth-century equivalent; Naipaul's Wiltshire is the perfection of literary solitude. The best that can be said of these resolutions, even on their own terms, is that they buy time and local relief in a deteriorating historical situation. The last novel in the sequence, *On Beauty*, presents no resolution at all, strictly speaking, closing in sight of transformations that are necessary but may never happen. Hardy inaugurates the other strong narrative tendency, in which the situation weighs more heavily from the outset. *Jude the Obscure* includes at least three (and, with Phillotson, four) failed transformations; Charles Ryder twice gains but then twice loses a foothold in the aristocracy; Ralph Kripalsingh's dreams of neo-classical coherence and order come to nothing; the situation in *A Kind of Loving* remains open, but few would bet much on Vic's chances of realizing his intellectual ambitions; Fred Clegg's fantasy of self-improvement is a horror to which all Miranda's defensive resourcefulness proves unequal, and his quest for cultural validation ends in the symbolic destruction of culture itself.

The Collector, along with *A Judgement in Stone*, forms a subset of narratives in which, contrariwise, an achieved social concentration of cultural value comes under attack from below and is destroyed. Compared with Rendell's novel, it is a hybrid: Fred's desire is a dangerous mutation of Jude's and Bast's, but he is descended from them nonetheless. The transformation he sets out to effect is self-betterment, not the death of the love-object, and he survives to reflect on the experience of his first initiative. Eunice Parchman, in contrast, is not in search of transformation, and least of all the kind of transformation that most matters to these seekers after culture. The life adjustments she makes after her father's death are all designed to safeguard an existing state of affairs, the secret of her illiteracy. In this, she complements Jacqueline Coverdale, who is likewise motivated by the desire to have things as they are, or rather, to put the finishing touch to the nearly perfect idyll of her cultivated, leisured existence. The transformation, if that is quite what it is, that occurs in *A Judgement in Stone* is unique in this series of narratives in resulting from the collision of two opposed situations, both of them intensely valued, one a cultural plenitude as narcissistically complete in its bourgeois way as Woolf's dream of aristocracy, the other its sterile proletarian negative. The social ascriptions call for emphasis, for this is a story of frontal class conflict, and the resulting 'transformation', anything but dialectical in character, looks more like the end of the world.

2

The main stake, throughout this series, is books and their uses. Fine art and architecture and music have defining roles in some important instances, but reading remains the dominant cultural mode, just as literature remains the touchstone of cultural competence and commitment, even where its context is an approaching end-state of post-literacy. (Television furnishes the stock antithesis from the 1950s onwards.) Libraries and other collections of cultural objects, including their immaterial equivalents in the encyclopaedic stores of individual and shared memories, are correspondingly regular features of these narratives, sometimes as plot-functions, more widely as indices of character and situation.

The books that Jude Fawley searches out are the necessary instruments of his aspiration to learning (as well as an index of its social incongruity, the will to pass from one kind of obscurity to another). Fred Clegg's purchases serve a parallel function in a deranged variation on this project. The books that fill the rooms of Lowfield Hall signify the precise class-fractional identity of the Coverdales, and also form an element of the cultural provocation that leads to their violent deaths. Charles Ryder, newly arrived in Oxford, declares himself in his personal cultural manifest: a mix of modern art and aesthetics and not-so-modern poetry, with a pronounced Bloomsbury accent – and a copy of Norman Douglas's *South Wind*.[4]

Libraries are at least as important for their modes of existence – formation, continuation, use – as for their citable contents. It is normal to associate books with shelves, and bookshelves with specialized rooms for reading, but this common sense is quickly dispelled by the evidence of these narratives, in which libraries acquire chronotopical value, as spatial forms (literal or notional) in which temporal relations – the historical trajectories of individuals, families and classes – are made concrete.[5] Thus, a pair of bookcases standing locked and keyless in a country house may suggest a whole narrative of inheritance and failing grasp in a

4   This is just one episode in *South Wind*'s literary afterlife as a stage property in other novels. Its cachet in the twenties and thirties (it was first published in 1917) may be judged from the fact that it was one of the first novels to be released in paperback in Britain (Penguin, 1935). It had already appeared as a test of moral sensibility in Elizabeth Bowen's *The Last September* (1929), set just a little before Charles's arrival in Oxford, and appears again, at the identical point in the self-disclosure of another new Oxford undergraduate, in Naipaul, *The Enigma of Arrival*. *Brideshead* in its turn appears in Rendell, *A Judgement in Stone*, as a character index for young Giles Mont, with his penchant for spiritual extremity.

5   M.M. Bakhtin, *The Dialogic Imagination: Four Essays*, Austin, 1981, pp. 84–258.

family or a whole class.[6] Hardy proposes one extreme variation. Jude's library is not 'a library' at all. He acquires his books with passion and difficulty, and never finds a reserved place for them. Arabella, coming across them on the kitchen table, dashes them to the floor where they will no longer be 'in the way'.[7] They find shelf-space for the first time in the room where he is laid out in death. Sue Bridehead keeps her books in her luggage, a 'library' scarcely less temporary than Jude's and also clandestine, because repugnant to the Christian ethos of the house where she lodges.

Among private libraries, the polar contrast with Jude's is that in Marchmain House, the Flyte family's London *palazzo*. It is a sarcophagus of a kind, 'the one ugly room in either of their houses', where no one ever sits, or opens the obsolete works of reference.[8] Between these extremes are ranged various realizations of 'the library'.[9] Shahid's collection, unlike Jude's or Sue's, has begun as an inheritance, a gift from his 'satirical' Uncle Asif, who thinks to pass on the broad, freethinking progressivism of his intellectual generation. A legacy, it is nevertheless an active one, for Asif himself is alive and his example has helped to form the habits of discrimination that Shahid brings to the conflicting cultural tendencies he encounters on moving to London. The library at Pointz Hall is also an inheritance that continues to

---

6   As in Bowen, *The Last September* (1929), London 1998, p. 10.

7   Hardy, *Jude the Obscure*, p. 114.

8   Waugh, *Brideshead Revisited*, p. 200.

9   But not the public institutions that might have compensated (and historically did). These are hardly to be seen at any date in this sequence. Eunice Parchman has visited a public library to return a book for a friend, and remembers it as a place of 'mystery and threat' (Rendell, *A Judgement in Stone*, p. 55). John Self begins to read, after his ruin, but values the local library mainly as a place of shelter (Amis, *Money*, p. 387).

grow, but according to a principle of degradation: an old deposit of cultivation progressively overlain by the literary refuse of train journeys.

Howards End is emblematic as an effort to reach a state of equipoise in the sphere of culture. Between Bast, the clerk whose will to transcendence is unmatched by the means to achieve it, and Henry Wilcox, the entrepreneur for whom bourgeois plenty is the means to more of the same, stand the Schlegel sisters, high-minded rentiers in whose lives culture as transcendence and culture as inherited sustaining environment are united. However, the ambivalences of Forster's construction are marked, and the library is their prime site. Bast is given to adding up his cultural activities like so many acquisitions, and in Margaret's opinion, clutters his brain 'with the husks of books, culture – horrible' – rather than 'the real thing'.[10] This will do as a pejorative summing-up of libraries and their users, a late-romantic commonplace quickly reaching the same terminus as simple philistinism. The contrary impulse turns out to lead in the same direction. Culture, for the Schlegels, is an ethos, not an accumulation of objects and events. But ethos, as environment, materializes as living-space and thus, by ineluctable association, as furniture and decoration. The Schlegel's library is a serious collection, but the room itself features only as a convenient place for delicate conversations.

Lowfield Hall, in contrast, has no such room. The whole house is 'full of books', the new housekeeper perceives, and 'they read books all the time', everywhere. These books are more than furniture, then, yet not the transforming resources that Jude and

---

10   Forster, *Howards End*, p. 137.

Sue and Bast seek out or the Schlegels find to hand. That is not what books are for at Lowfield. The Coverdales' reading habit is predominantly phatic: not critical, rather affirmative of their life together, more sweetness than light.

Martin Amis posits an antithetical cultural condition. Anything but cultivated, his protagonist is a self-styled 'yob'. Neither he nor Selina ever reads. 'Culture and all that – it's not, or not only, that we aren't cut out for it, some of us. We sort of hate it too.'[11] Transcendence has all but vanished from the London and Manhattan of the early 1980s, and the culture that instantiated it has been refunctioned as branding material or a leisure option. Yet its traces are everywhere. Self's world is a whispering gallery of famous names from four or more national literatures. This wholesale transmigration of souls from literature to signage is one form of the final subsumption of culture under capital, a process whose teasing visible effect is that the streets of a post-literate metropolis come more and more to resemble the venue for some great book festival, or a library of sorts.

3

Libraries, in their turn, function as prominent elements of the larger topic of the house. To a remarkable degree, this is a tradition of novels about houses. Two take their titles from the names of houses (*Howards End* and *Brideshead Revisited*) and a third, published posthumously as *Between the Acts*, normally appeared in Virginia Woolf's diary as *PH* (for Pointz Hall). In most of them, houses and their histories are a major narrative

---

11   Amis, *Money*, p. 387.

interest,[12] variously related to the central concern with cultural evaluation. In one group of novels, the history of the house is a simple index of a cultural state of affairs. The mock-Roman villa that Ralph Kripalsingh builds for himself after his return to Isabella is a material illustration of the vanity of postcolonial aspiration: his adult life begins in a London boarding house and comes to a mid-life stasis in a London hotel. Lowfield Hall is the embodiment of the Coverdales' cultural plenty. The sale of Deedee Osgood's marital home – 'a large family house', in the real-estate jargon mimicked here, but with no children and now no husband, only lodgers – signifies the disintegration of a certain left-wing cultural-political milieu in London in the 1980s.[13] Howards End, in contrast, is not so much an index as a test. Value inheres in the house as the material form of moral continuity with Mrs Wilcox and her farming forebears and the England they are taken to incarnate. *Be worthy of this place!* is the plea of the novel – and not the least of the meanings of its famous motto, 'Only connect'. Orlando's great house is a value in much the same sense, a collective, inter-generational work whose care and maintenance are a quasi-artistic achievement in themselves. In *Brideshead*, Charles Ryder brings this trope to fulfilment, fusing culture and property in the form of architecture. His summer at the house is 'an aesthetic education',[14] and he finds his *métier* at last as an 'architectural artist', a painter of property.

12 Reciprocally, there are novels of houses that cross the territory of the novel of culture: Waugh's *A Handful of Dust* (1934), to which *Brideshead* stands as an elegiac reparative gesture, a palinode of sorts, is one such; Bowen's *The Heat of the Day* is a more striking case.

13 Kureishi, *The Black Album*, p. 39.

14 Waugh, *Brideshead Revisited*, p. 78.

As chronotope, the house readily accommodates the great topics of cultural history and judgement: continuity and severance, rise and (more often) decline. In the London of Forster and Waugh, the demolition crews are busy. The Schlegels' family home in Wickham Place is to be torn down to make way for a block of flats and Marchmain House is levelled for the same purpose.[15] Howards End and Brideshead, meanwhile, are sites of a crisis in continuity. Henry Wilcox sees little point in his wife's old home: it is 'inconvenient'. Who will have Brideshead, and to what good long-term end, is the governing question of Waugh's novel, which offers no positive historical answer. Even Orlando's house has its phase of crisis. The outcomes are various, but with a tendency to the worse, especially in the later history. Lowfield Hall goes to ruin after the slaughter of the Coverdales, 'a bleak house' for its time. The manor house at the centre of *The Enigma of Arrival* continues its long decline. The Osgood-Brownlow house is torched by a working-class drug-dealer. Ralph ends up in exile, Shahid and Deedee on the road, John Self just a step from skid row – all, by the received standard, homeless.

It is the sentimental charge of inheritance that spiritualizes the material facts of survival and conveyance, rendering the house so potent as a trope of continuity. Mrs Wilcox represents the moral bond of property in its strongest sense: she 'belongs to the house' – not it to her – 'and to the tree that overshadowed it', and in this shows 'that wisdom to which we give the

---

15   See also Waugh's *A Handful of Dust*, in which Beaver's mother has subdivided a townhouse into small flats – dressing rooms and love nests rather than places to live – and then note the contrast with *A Judgement in Stone*, in which Eunice freely abandons her family home to demolition.

clumsy name of aristocracy'.[16] This is a telling attribution, in the strictly bourgeois world of *Howards End*, indicating what really is central in *Orlando* and in *Brideshead*: aristocratic property as the material guarantee of cultural continuity. Lowfield Hall, in contrast, is no Howards End, let alone Brideshead. George's inheritance is his father's tin box factory, and his culture has come through formal education. The manor house is a recent acquisition, and he and Jacqueline have 'slipped into playing the parts of the squire and his wife'.[17] George's purchase is a rarity among these stories of houses. Renting is normal, as a likely concomitant of class situation (Jude, Bast) or transitional status (Shahid as student, or the migrant narrator of *The Enigma of Arrival*), and increasingly as an ontological condition of modernity that is already manifest in Henry Wilcox and reaches its furthest generality in John Self. The only exception deserves note. Fred Clegg prepares his seventeenth-century cottage as the place to receive his cultured 'guest'. Like George Coverdale, he has bought his house, but not in the ordinary way of the affluent; he owes it to his big win on the pools. For the self-conscious cultural minoritarian Miranda, his efforts are vulgar and inept – and frightening. The heritage, in Fred's keeping, becomes its own prison.

4

The moment of culture – of transcendence towards another self or situation – is conditioned by crisis in the plane of family relations. Most of the protagonists of these narratives are orphans,

---

16   Forster, *Howards End*, p. 22.
17   Rendell, *A Judgement in Stone*, p. 8.

and where parents survive, they fail as instances of the authority and nurture the family order ideally guarantees. Hardy discloses Jude's aloneness in the same narrative movement that sees his ambition take shape. The Brown House barn, where, in his infancy, his mother and father parted for the last time, is also the spot where he has his first vision of the university town of Christminster. There 'shall be my Alma Mater: and I'll be her beloved son, in whom she shall be well pleased' – mother, and father too, as the scriptural allusion suggests.[18] The Schlegel sisters' orphan state is hardly a cause of crisis; they live as rentier intellectuals with a degree of autonomy rare in women of their age and class. But Margaret has begun to wonder whether the stock reflexes of 'culture' are the truths they are taken to be – and Bast's orphanhood, in contrast, is a condition in which rootlessness combines with poverty to render life yet more precarious and aspiration still more fallible. For Charles Ryder, the motherless son of a whimsical, distracted antiquary, it is the pull of 'what I had never known, a happy childhood', that draws him beyond his first, 'intellectual' attachments into the sublimated social world of Brideshead-as-art.[19] Fred Clegg has lost both parents and the uncle who raised him. As he embarks on his project, he is, at last, alone. His 'guest', for her part, has psychically over-written her parents – who are alive – in a family romance, substituting first an 'artistic' aunt and now a boorish *Übermensch*, the painter G.P.[20] For Shahid, the death of the father is an existential crux. The house 'where his father no longer was' turns 'anarchic' and

---

18   Hardy, *Jude the Obscure*, p. 80. Cf. Matthew 3:17.

19   Waugh, *Brideshead Revisited*, p. 45.

20   A crude interpretive key, this: Miranda's father is in general medical practice, or, in British parlance, a GP.

he must withdraw from the family 'to think about their lives and why they had come to England'.[21]

Where the family is structurally complete, on the other hand, the hour of culture never strikes. Arabella is immoveable in her attachment to her family and the common sense of their class. Of the four interwoven biographies that make up *Jude the Obscure*, only hers omits the theme of self-transcendence, and only she survives intact. In the same way, Henry Wilcox remains immoveable in his fidelity to the calling of bourgeois patriarch, obtuse enough to strike a 'chill' into the visionary finale of *Howards End*. The Belsey family is stressed by the academic self-engrossment of a very different father-figure, himself half-estranged from his own father in London, and the unanswered question of *On Beauty* is whether Howard and Kiki will share the family home again.

In all these novels, culture and family are projected as contraries, or alternatives. In another variation, they appear as mutuals, or as moments of a unity. *Orlando* figures the immanence of culture in class, a whole line of 'fathers' (the plural is marked, and the line has no beginning, for they 'had been noble since they had been at all'), which Orlando eventually joins, continuing a process of creative parthenogenesis in which culture and family are symbolically the same.[22] The Coverdales present a bourgeois variation on this ideal fusion. The family is in itself, indeed, an achievement of culture, for George and Jacqueline, with no child of their own, have created it, after bereavement and divorce, out

---

21 Kureishi, *The Black Album*, pp. 21–2, 6.

22 Woolf, *Orlando*, p. 9. *Brideshead* narrates the counter-case of an aristocratic family, women as well as men this time, who fail to sustain the culture (the house and the lineage) they have inherited.

of their previous marriages. Bourgeois family: bourgeois culture: the symbiosis is ideal while it lasts. However, there remains one further variation, in which there are only minus signs. Elsewhere, a working-class family has ended, releasing a force antithetical to culture. Eunice Parchman has foreclosed her invalid father's lease on life and now needs a place where she can continue to evade the demands of a literate society. She gives up her parents' house for demolition and, saying a last goodbye to her 'kind neighbour', her 'near mother', sets off for a new job and a new, unthreatening life at Lowfield Hall.

Without effective fathers, the line of inter-generational authority is cut, and surrogate relations, transverse rather than lineal, become a norm. These are never successful in their own terms. Aunts, maiden or widowed, do their insufficient best. Great-aunt Drusilla, the gloomy bard of the Fawleys, tries to steer Jude away from the family doom, but unavailingly. The benevolent, fussing Mrs Munt is no match for the Schlegels and the *genius loci* of Howards End. Charles Ryder's Aunt Phillipa despairs of her widowed brother's perversities and withdraws, leaving behind her only a dining protocol and a bundle of menus. Fred Clegg chafes under Aunt Annie's austere Christian tutelage, and Miranda soon wearies of her aunt Caroline's affectations. Cousins appear as active disciplinarians. Jasper presumes to advise Charles and then to have him brought to book. Aunt Annie's daughter Mabel urges stricter enforcement of the family's Nonconformist rules. The great exception is of course Sue Bridehead. But Sue is not, functionally speaking, the same kind of figure as these helper/hinderer aunts and cousins: the authority she acquires over Jude is the special, charismatic authority that inheres in the status of the beloved. In *Orlando* and *A Judgement in Stone*, such transverse authority figures have no place: these are narratives of plenitude, aristocratic and bourgeois respectively, even if only one of them turns out to be future-proof. *The Black Album*, by contrast, is the novel in which transversality becomes a general norm, as Shahid's family disintegrates. Here, the contention of authorities becomes the organizing principle and matter of the narrative.

Sprung from the crisis of a family, these projects of transcendence often inscribe their goal in the constitution of a new one. The crisis of *A Kind of Loving* occurs at the very moment of transition from a settled working-class family to a new home, which may just accommodate something of Vic's cultural priorities but is more likely to be organized around Ingrid's trivial pastimes. Pregnancy and childbirth are inevitably central here, both as the literal natural means of continuity and as a tropology of narrative evaluation and conjecture in the planes of society and culture. The eventual arrival of a male heir suggests that Orlando's completed being will reproduce itself to noble infinity. Helen Schlegel's untimely pregnancy precipitates the final crisis of the old bourgeois dispensation and sets the terms of an adjusted one: Howards End will pass not to Charles Wilcox's children but to Leonard Bast's – or rather, to the intellectuals who will raise his son as one of themselves. Likewise, Louie's elevation to motherhood, through a mishap rendered blameless by the accidents of wartime, gives early warning of the culture of the generation to come. Such narrative turns are not only predictive, of course: they often illustrate the common-sense probabilities of the situation in which they occur. A deceitful claim of pregnancy is the ploy by which Arabella tricks Jude into marriage, so putting an end to the first phase of his struggle for education, and a real but belated conception produces the strange boy (Jude the younger, or Little Time) whose grim depressive reasoning opens the way to the catastrophic last act of the novel. In a later period, similarly, Ingrid's accidental pregnancy condemns Vic to wedlock at a point where he no longer values their relationship; and the relief of a miscarriage comes too late to save him from a future with a woman who cannot share his intellectual interests. One possible outcome of Shahid's life with Deedee has been prefigured in another such accident, from his teens, this one ending in an abortion and the disruption of his plans for further study. It is evident that these are not only tropes of reproduction; their significance is more general, forming part of a quite regular gendering of cultural probabilities.

The search for culture is masculine. It is not that men are confined to this narrative function, but that they monopolize it. Jude, Bast, Charles, Clegg, the Naipaul figure in Wiltshire, Shahid: these are the seekers in their respective stories – and it is as his younger, male self that Orlando turns to Greene for guidance; by the time of their second, accidental encounter she is a fulfilment of cultural possibility, the poet of *The Oak Tree*, or English literature. This change of role captures a basic feature in the patterning of the genre as a whole. If women do not search for culture, they may nevertheless embody it, as do Sue, Margaret and Helen, Julia, Miranda, Jacqueline, Martina and Deedee, giving it an erotically charged authority. However, there is one proviso: women who are not already established in this positive role at their point of entry into the present time of the narrative will appear antithetically, as hindering, distracting presences at least, and at the limit, figures of simple negation. Arabella, Jackie, Louie, Eunice and Selina are imagined at, or very near, that limit. The idea that they might become searchers is unintelligible: not merely lacking in cultural attainment or aspiration, they are forces of resistance, embodiments of the anti-cultural principle. Their characteristic power is sexual.[23] Arabella diverts Jude from study and actively discourages his attempts to resume; Bast puts his book away to answer the insistent call from the bedroom; Vic allows his sexual weakness for Ingrid to compromise his cultural desire; Selina sets up an erotic spectacle to see off the superior Martina, who is John's one faint hope of a change of life. Vee Kipps is hardly unculturable, but her specialized plot function in *On Beauty* is to turn the heads of men of culture and disrupt their plans.

Sue and Deedee, at the beginning and the end of this historical sequence, are complex in this regard, escaping the dichotomous organization of women in culture, being both authoritative embodiments of culture and sexually attractive. They differ from the others in that they seek to live their personal lives, whether erotically accented or not, in keeping with articulate principle. The distraction they incarnate is one from a received authority to a new and higher norm. Each in her own way and in her generation an emancipated intellectual, both women figure moments of strain in the sexist imaginary of the condition of culture novel. Sue's challenge to orthodoxy is much the greater offence, and the narrative recuperation, when it comes, is brutal; in Deedee's case, a century later, there is only the lingering suggestion that her revolution has dwindled into consumerism. But Joan Smith, with her paranoid evangelism and a scandalous sexual history

---

23 Eunice is the stark exception: it is as if an ordinary endowment of sexuality has been transferred from her to Joan along with the expected measure of literacy.

including a phase of prostitution, is the travesty version of their aspirations, a figure suggesting that such exceptional cases turn out to be little different from the common run of unculturable women.

5

The culture men seek is feminine, as also is the anti-cultural power that diverts them from their purpose, and sometimes the two are one and the same. This is the genre's individual variation on the old symbolic antitheses of the madonna and the whore. There are complicating instances, indeed, but they remain equivocal: the marvellous Orlando aside, there is no female character in the century-long sequence who escapes this shaping fixation.

Symbolically charged in this way, the image of culture projected in these novels is also marked as national. There are qualifications to be made. Hardy's early critical excursus on the wanton 'improvement' of English church architecture is, precisely, a digression, not sustained enough to modify the semantics of his novel as a whole; the history of the genre overall is not, in respect of the nation, the record of uniformity that its gendering of culture so strikingly illustrates; and some of the novels do not figure at all. Nevertheless, there is a significant continuity of attachment, and Forster's appeal to England and Englishness, at its most intense in the visionary nineteenth chapter of *Howards End*, resonates for decades. There, at a vantage-point high in the Purbeck Hills, 'the reason fails' and 'the imagination swells, spreads and deepens, until it becomes geographic and encircles England'.[24] This transfiguring cultural value is England in its

---

24   Forster, *Howards End*, p. 157.

imputed difference from imperial Britain, which is the mainstay of Wilcoxes, but also in its difference from cosmopolitanism, which is what the Schlegels move beyond, in a narrative that takes them from a London street to a hayfield in Hertfordshire. The enigmatic token of cultural continuity in that novel is the wych-elm at Howards End; Orlando's special tree is a solitary oak growing on high ground in the parkland around the great house. This is in the first place a metaphor for his narcissistic will to completeness. It is also the master-trope of his reprise of English literature, and a conventional emblem of English-ness itself. And literally, however improbably, it marks a place from which, on a clear day, he can see all of England and beyond. Brideshead too is a magical place, as it seems to Charles Ryder on his unexpected return in wartime, and the world from which it promises pastoral respite is doubly distinct: the raw margins of Glasgow, where he has spent the past desolate months, are both modern – 'the extreme limit of the city', as he puts it[25] – and un-English.

This pastoral note is seldom sounded after 1945, but homages to the national-cultural continue, most strikingly in the form of semi-cryptic naming practices. 'George Paston', the full name of G.P. in *The Collector*, replicates the form of another, much revered patriotic coinage, 'George Orwell', in all its elements and with the same connotative purpose, it seems, combining the national saint's name with a family name signifying association with the local landscape (Orwell) and social history (Paston) of East Anglia.[26] Elsewhere in the same region of England, another

---

25   Waugh, *Brideshead Revisited*, p. 9.

26   The Paston family were Norfolk gentry associated with the village of the same name. They are remembered for the extensive correspondence

George and his wife discharge the responsibilities of affluent, literate Anglicans in keeping with the example of their nominal ancestor, Coverdale the bible-maker.[27] In such cases, where identity and function merge, the signature doubles as a dedication and unremarkable proper names assume the abstract power of allegory.

'England' in Forster was an available cultural grace and a haven for the liberal conscience; the Woolf of *Orlando* could affirm it as a zone of fulfilment, in the mode of fantasy; Waugh too could retrieve it, though only as the memory of a lost paradise. There is nothing left of that receding pastoral in *The Collector* or *A Judgement in Stone*: G.P. and Miranda are self-consciously at battle stations and the peace of Lowfield Hall is illusory. With the opening of the era of decolonization and the quickening, ramifying streams of inward migration, the received idea of the national-cultural virtue became complicated, or aporetic, and in the first place suspect. Forster's distinction between England and Britain, which translated a discrepancy between culture and commercial self-interest or between personal loyalties and Realpolitik, could not be sustained in the colonies, where certain styles of Englishness were culturally dominant in the formula of British rule. For Naipaul in *The Mimic Men* and *The Enigma of*

---

that survived them, dating from the fifteenth century and attracting significant scholarly attention from the 1700s onwards ('the Paston Letters'). The River Orwell is in the neighbouring county of Suffolk.

27　It is impossible to overlook T. S. Eliot's contribution – the first, as it may be – to this arcane tradition of cultural loyalism. The lexicographical motto in his *Notes Towards the Definition of Culture* (1948), concerning the desirable 'limitation' of culture, is dated 1483, the year in which the Yorkist King Edward IV died: a dark moment for his dynasty, which was toppled two years later, so severing the English royal line.

Arrival, 'England' is an internalized command that has invalidated the local cultural codes of home, severed the umbilical cord to ancestral lineages of feeling, and, as a deadly culminating blow in the altered conditions of the post-war years, withdrawn its magical promise of order and wholeness – withdrawn it from itself, as it were, as well as from the assorted newcomers from the colonies and elsewhere. The hopeless truth of national culture, be it grand and faded or 'emerging', is that of alienated, degraded and probably futile routines. The London boarding house is the epitome of post-imperial Britain, and the minutely studied West Country neighbours who form the society of *The Enigma of Arrival* are 'campers in the ruins', in their way as much remnants as the famous antiquities that surround them; they are human fragments of England after 'England', illustrating no coherent history – collectively, an animated archaeology of the present.

Naipaul is held by an idea of England that has no habitable referent – and never had one, for an Indian from Trinidad, so that nostalgia is unavailable even as a placebo. His postcolonial melancholy is *Kulturkritik* at an extreme of existential nihilism. Kureishi's London, by contrast, is a historical situation full of constraint and danger but also energizing uncertainties – Shahid has looked forward to going there, 'dreaming of how rough and mixed [it] would be' (3). But here too, amidst the politics and music and drugs of the late twentieth century, the theme of decline is sounded in familiar terms: the degeneration of the working class is itself a deferred action from English literary history, with a new species named in advance by H.G. Wells (the Morlocks) and a ubiquitous, all-seeing Shakespearean commentator, in the person of the drug-dealer Strapper, christened 'Stratford'. Zadie

Smith's paeans to North-West London are little enough to set against this record of historical dismay.

6

The desolation of Lowfield Hall is the most complete cultural rupture in a sequence of novels in which failing continuity or the threat of it is commonplace. *Jude the Obscure* is virtually alone in the earlier decades in entertaining the possibility that there might be a progressive tendency in history, and *A Kind of Loving* is similarly isolated in the post-war phase. *Howards End* combines reforming sympathies with a conventional vision of the modern decline – suburban creep, motor cars and luggage – of the kind that the journal *Scrutiny* would render programmatic and polemical twenty years later, in the 1930s. Cars and other future-bearing novelties are welcome in *Orlando*, which nevertheless remains fortified against modern social classes, and in *Between the Acts* it seems that life at Pointz Hall has gone beyond mere cultural entropy to wholesale civilizational regress.

These are assorted indications. It is only from the 1940s, with Waugh's annunciation of the Age of Hooper, that the significant regularities of novelistic cultural evaluation become evident, in a series of parallels with the essayistic *Kulturkritik* of the time. Bowen's character Louie might be a sketch drawn to illustrate F.R. Leavis's critique of 'mass civilization'.[28] Barstow's appraisal of working-class life in industrial Lancashire ranges across a cultural landscape very like that of Richard Hoggart's *The Uses*

---

28   Leavis's *Mass Civilization and Minority Culture* was published in 1930. He was the inspirational editor of the quarterly *Scrutiny* for most of its lifetime (1932–1953).

of Literacy, though with greater attention to the workplace, and, in the characters of Ingrid and her mother, concretizes a similar alarm at the rising tides of the mass market in entertainment.[29] Fowles's defence of 'the Few' against 'the monied masses' updates Lawrentian cultural criticism for a new period, while bidding strongly to establish a new standard for phobic invective in the manner of Orwell.[30]

Hoggart, Barstow and Fowles were all to one degree or another left-leaning in politics, and some two decades after *A Judgement in Stone*, Ruth Rendell entered the British House of Lords as an official Labour nominee and self-styled socialist.[31] However, her novelistic cultural criticism places her squarely on the right, in the company of the arch-conservative T. S. Eliot. Cultivation and illiteracy have long coexisted without incident in

---

29   Hoggart's book (London, 1957, and originally to have been called 'the *ab*uses of literacy') drew on his experience of Yorkshire, notably the cities of Leeds and Hull, whereas Barstow's setting was based on the Manchester area. Barstow's novel can also be read as providing support for Richard Wollheim's critical evaluation of family as the spinal value, conservative and conformist, in British working-class culture. See Wollheim's *Socialism and Culture*, Fabian Tract 331, London, 1961, pp. 12–13.

30   For Lawrence on 'the moneyboy and the moneygirl', see *Lady Chatterley's Lover* (1928), Ch. 9. Fowles exploited the great success of *The Collector* to publish a personal cultural manifesto, *The Aristos* (London, 1964; the title-word is singular, pronounced áristos, meaning 'the best in the circumstances'), with the revealing sub-title 'a self-portrait in ideas'. Compare the manner of Miranda's social invective also with George Orwell's notorious tirade in *The Road to Wigan Pier* (respectively, *The Collector*, p. 207, and Orwell, London, 1937, p. 206).

31   'I'm a socialist, I'm Labour and always have been', she wrote, at the death of her fellow peer (Conservative) and crime novelist P. D. James ('Everything could have happened in her novels', *Guardian*, 28 November 2014) – an association of ideas as familiar and as tenacious as it is discredited.

the rural England of the novel; hard manual work and childbear-
ing have been occupation enough for the villagers. Low-level
class friction turns to something much more dangerous only
with the introduction of two aggravating factors. The first is a
specific educational surplus: not the Coverdales', whose household culture is simply the finest bloom of their social status, but
Joan's – Joan, whose unruly appetite for reading is the fruit of
her schooling, in which she has over-achieved. The second is
personal mobility. Eunice (like Joan) is a recent arrival from the
big city, a proletarian lacking any sense of continuity in her life.
She is content with television and chocolate, but the Coverdales,
in keeping with their general paternalism, make the mistake of
trying to improve her. These are the particular conditions that
bring on the disaster – which, then, appears as a lurid negative
confirmation of the kind of cultural wisdom proffered in Eliot's
Notes Towards the Definition of Culture. 'Definition', in that book,
meant 'limitation' or 'restriction', as a positive cultural good in
a hierarchical social order. And 'on the whole', he wrote there,
'it would appear to be for the best that the great majority of
human beings should go on living in the place in which they were
born'.[32] Just so.

Forster, Woolf and Waugh, Bowen, Barstow and Fowles
narrate different intensities of decline or crisis; Rendell imagines
the moment of catastrophe; others, clustered towards the later
end of this series of novels, presuppose the loss of continuity
or the capacity for transcendence, and then work through the

---

32   T. S. Eliot, *Notes Towards the Definition of Culture*, London, 1962,
p. 52. For relevant discussions of Eliot, and also Leavis and Hoggart, among
others, see my *Culture/Metaculture*.

minor narratives (they cannot be 'grand',[33] even at small scale) that a foreclosed condition allows. Amis offers one such narrative in *Money*, an incident-filled picaresque in the dead end of commodified barbarism. Fat Vince and Martina are ineffectual residues, proletarian and patrician respectively, of an order now past, and Martin, through the agency of his vicarious real-world namesake, is reduced, like Nabokov's ape, to drawing the bars of his cage.[34] Naipaul's historical waste land is far greater in temporal and spatial extent: it covers most of the earth and has been more than five centuries in the making. Over that time, the fundamental process of European empire-building, followed by the much more rapid phase of decolonization, has been one of progressive and irreparable cultural self-estrangement leading to an end-state of mimicry, from which the only redemption is a narcissistic ethic of writing in which narrative gives birth to itself – a bohemian continuation of Woolf's aristocratic fantasy of transcendence. It is not clear whether, obeying the same logic of withdrawal, *The Black Album* is the work that Shahid begins to write as the novel comes to a close, and it is also unclear whether the relevant cultural continuities are damaged beyond retrieval. Popular existence has been devastated by economic decline, racism and drugs, and the left is a ruin. The idea of enlightenment that Shahid has inherited is doubly challenged, in one way by young zealots who excoriate it as rootless apostasy, in another by his lover whose personal disposition is a fading simulacrum of youth culture. Kureishi's novel (like *On Beauty* in this respect) is designedly a continuing story, but the prospects are not good.

---

33   'Grand', that is, in the way of Jean-François Lyotard's *grands récits*.

34   Vladimir Nabokov, 'On a Book Entitled *Lolita*' (1956), *Lolita*, London: 1961, p. 328.

7

Social classes are central to the condition of culture novel, and above all the working class, which Kureishi pictures at a moment of historic moral crisis. In *The Black Album*, something has come to an end. Set in a recent and dated past, the novel nevertheless has the air of aftermath familiar from near-future narratives. And what has ended is British Labourism – what was understood for much of the twentieth century, by its loyal working-class adherents and their enemies alike, as a mass political movement towards some kind of socialism. In this respect as in others, Kureishi's novel is characteristic of the English condition of culture novel, whose course, over the century from *Jude the Obscure* to *The Black Album*, appears to track that of the labour movement and the wider working class, offering a commentary on it.

Jude and *Howards End*, dating from the last years of the nineteenth century and the first decade of the twentieth, belong to the formative period of the modern labour movement, the decades that saw the growth of new general unions, the creation of the Labour Party itself, and the emergence of independent institutions of working-class education. The cultural perspectives governing these initiatives were a matter of open controversy in the years when Forster was writing his novel, and it is, then, the more noteworthy that, for all the relative benignity of treatment, almost nothing is made of the institutional settings, new and no longer new, of working-class adult learning, of which he at least had first-hand experience (as a tutor). Both Jude and Bast are isolates, imagined in that way as one aspect of their construction as tragic subjects whose projects must fail. Jude eventually joins an artisans' study group only to be eased out because of his scandalous living arrangements, and Bast remains a lonely, awkward autodidact.[35] Culture proves the death of them. Jude leaves no living children, and the infant Bast, anticipating the general politico-cultural experience of his class, will be taken in hand by Fabians. Either way, the effort of self-education comes to exactly nothing.

In *Orlando* such matters never arise. The chronology of the fiction happily disinvents modern social classes for much of the narrative, and older forms of labour, chiefly domestic in focus and pseudo-familial in ethos, predominate throughout.[36] *Brideshead Revisited* organizes a parallel regression, though in social rather than historical terms. The principal settings are those in which, again, pseudo-familial forms of labour predominate: nannies, butlers, college servants. Oxford's 'proletarian' scholars are heard of, but not seen, and in the chapter devoted to the General Strike of 1926 the tone is comic. Charles and his fellow-strikebreakers see very little of their class enemy, whose reality is perhaps open to question after all – 'It was as though a beast long fabled for its ferocity had emerged for an hour, scented danger and slunk back to its lair.'[37] The older Charles who narrates this episode nearly twenty years later senses danger, and specifically

---

35   Jonathan Rose's study *The Intellectual Life of the British Working Class* (New Haven and London, 2001) provides essential, wide-ranging historical context: see especially the chapter 'What Was Leonard Bast Really Like?', pp. 393–438.

36   In fact, the rise of the organized working class set the tone in the 1920s, even if its political victories were less impressive than its defeats. Woolf herself participated in her local Party branch in rural Sussex (along with two of her own employees) from late 1931. See Alison Light, *Mrs Woolf and the Servants*, London, 2007.

37   Waugh, *Brideshead Revisited*, p. 199.

an imminent cultural threat, but its bearer is nothing so romantic as 'Red revolution', merely the social blur named Hooper.

Nineteen-forty-five, the year the Labour Party came to office with a landslide majority, is a symbolic turning point in the history of the culture novel. This was a moment such as Waugh had been dreading – worse again, perhaps – and a departure that came to the wartime democrat Bowen as a 'terrific' and literally sickening 'psychic shock'.[38] With *The Heat of the Day*, Louie joins Hooper as an avatar of the mass cultural subject – Louie and her son, whose home will be the cultural antitype of Howards End and whose name is Victor, or 'winner'. Winning is variably construed over the next decade. It may refer to the general yield of welfare and full employment as this is evaluated in *A Kind of Loving*: an ambiguous state of cultural affairs, full of threat as well as promise, but still open. On the other hand, winning can take the freakish, implicitly dubious form of Fred Clegg's coup on the football pools, a result that is democratic inasmuch as any player might have won but that by definition cannot be classed as just or deserved. On this demonstration, the upshot of the post-war settlement is a plain cultural negative: the moneyed masses hold sway, to the worsening, potentially lethal, detriment of the Few.

---

38   'I can't stick all these little middle-class Labour wets with their Old London School of Economics ties and their women', she wrote to William Plomer in September 1945. 'Scratch any of these cuties and you find the governess. Or so I have always found.' (*The Mulberry Tree: Writings of Elizabeth Bowen*, ed. Hermione Lee, London, 1998.) Some months later, in a letter to Randolph Churchill, Waugh expressed his hope of buying a castle in Ireland, as 'brief shelter from the Atlee terror'. (*Letters of Evelyn Waugh*, London: Phoenix, 2010.) See Lara Feigel, *The Love-Charm of Bombs: Restless Lives in the Second World War*, London, 2013, pp. 280, 309 and 337 respectively.

Fifteen years and two Labour governments later, the relative merits of these contrasting assessments were rather clearer. In the world of *A Judgement in Stone*, bourgeois families continue to benefit from an expanded education system (Melinda's university is a new one, unlike her father's) and something of the associated social ethos survives among them, though in a paternalist rather than an egalitarian vein. But the evidence of the popular classes tells a different story. The villagers go on in their old, incorrigible way; of the two characters of London working-class origins, one is armoured against the printed word while the other is hyper-actively literate, and both are threatening, either refusing the constructive suggestions of their bourgeois betters or lawlessly monitoring their every move. Fred Clegg's fantasy of self-improvement has caused the death of a young woman, and that should be horror enough, but Eunice and Joan destroy a whole way of life. A half-century after Charles's romantic excursion in the General Strike, the advantage has passed to the other side. The fabled beast of red revolution has returned on more favourable social terrain and set about its work of devastation.

In the background of this paranoid allegory of class struggle were the international convulsions of 1968–1969 and, in Britain, the major workplace battles of the next decade. The fictional climax coincided closely with the real-world struggles in the factories, hospitals and coalfields, as the matter of winning (or losing) assumed a far graver form. Rendell projected coming disaster and asked, in the form of a narrative heavy with anticipation, whether it might have been averted; at about the same time, the British Conservative Party, under its new leader, Margaret Thatcher, was embarking on a mission to ensure that there would be no repeat of the early '70s. Ten years later, the militant rearguards of the labour movement had been defeated; the horror of the new period, as promptly imaged by Martin Amis, would be the universal dominion of money. It is to the political and workplace struggles of the 1970s and '80s that Kureishi's Brownlow and Deedee Osgood look back in *The Black Album*, but their memories are the only registration of those once-commanding realities to be found henceforward in the condition of culture novel. Howard Belsey's youthful experiences, which are of approximately the same vintage, are already more detached – the memories are of squatted houses, and 'the working class' is little more than a social provenance to be flaunted at 'Marxist conferences'.[39] Latterly, his campaigning energies have been channelled into the politics of affirmative action, 'the culture wars'. It is perhaps telling, then – it is certainly apt – that the conflict between two London intellectuals, Howard and Monty, in a novel that wears its home-town patriotism on its sleeve, should be transposed to the United States and scripted on terms that are more American than British.[40] There is historical sense in *On Beauty*'s awkwardness of fit in this series. In its internal dislocation it marks what looks like the end of the constitutive tradition of the English condition of culture novel, its old preoccupation with a labour movement now (2005) disarmed and half-dispersed.

Domestic class relations have not been the exclusive social focus of the genre, of course: the crises of postcoloniality have formed a second major topic at least since the 1950s. This is very clearly the dominant in Naipaul's work, where it governs the

---

39   Smith, *On Beauty*, p. 292.

40   As Rob Higney has observed, the Kippsian intellectual type is historically American, not British.

construction of class and also race, and crucial also in the complex narrative articulations of Kureishi and Smith – *On Beauty* especially, with its specific focus on the trans-national class relations of migrant labour. Still less has the genre monopolized fictional reflection on matters of class, which remain a staple of the English novel more broadly viewed. Nevertheless, the condition of culture novel has for a century and more persisted as a complex of narrative conventions by or through which, across a variety of social identifications, a literate middle class could frame or crop, acknowledge, consider and (more often than not) resist the active historical presence of the working class. The oldest and, arguably, most intractable constituent structure of social classes is the division of mental and manual labour, and differing levels of cultural capability – the distinction between the educated and the rest – have long served as a substitute reference for the plain realities of property and work, the more commonly once the idea of social mobility became an official desideratum. The constitutive problem of the genre has been that of culture, above all, the uses and abuses of literacy, and just how fraught and dangerous a zone of existence that is these novels make luridly explicit, in a century-long catalogue of hardship, heartbreak, violence and suffering unto death. Death for those who seek culture and death for those who have it: the outcome is not always so drastic, but overall this genre is the form in which *Kultur* – inwardness, sensibility, sweetness and light – turns into nightmare, a bad dream with the most general social implications. Cultural attachments pass over into forms of family and other personal relations and then, via their association with that psychically supercharged capital asset, the house, acquire the unyielding categorical forms of property and money. Learning – the desire for it, its processes and purposes – is a correspondingly heavily coded activity, a condensed, changeable trope of social self-assertion, challenge or demand, or any mix of these. It functions in the culture novel as an individualizing trope of social uncertainty – 'restlessness' is Hardy's significant word, encompassing both a personal state and more general dissatisfactions. The will to learn is sustained by the thought of other lives, but how and by whom those lives will be lived, with what implications for familiar ways – whether they will be lived at all, come to that – is unknown. The work of this genre, an Aristotelian might say, has been to manage the response to such social uncertainty, to express and purge the pity and the terror it may arouse. Its multiform extremism testifies to the force of the anxieties in play. The ambitions of Jude and Bast may be recognized, but only as tragedy, and, *per contra*, the mock-aristocratic insouciance of a Waugh is shadowed by melancholy and the dread of what may be coming. Orlando may embrace the servants in the mode retro of pastoral, but the goodwill of a civilized employer is wasted on the likes of Eunice Parchman – who, on the other hand, is an easy mark for a crazed agitator. Even the epochal triumph of money is entered to the discredit of those with little enough of it, a working class transfigured by the evasive trope of 'consumerism' into a yob army of capital.[41]

And anyway, it is not as if a productive reconciliation of culture and the working class seems possible on any terms at all, if these novels are to be believed. Such people pursue culture in

----

41 See, most recently, Martin Amis's *Lionel Asbo: State of England* (2012), a facile satire with a protagonist uniting John Self's most vicious qualities and Fred Clegg's fabulous good luck (handsomely adjusted for a half-century's inflation), the whole delivered in a mock-phonetic travesty of popular (Midlands) speech.

eccentric, wrong-headed schemes and, once offered it, either recoil or find their place in a spectrum of abuse extending from the trivial to the monstrous, with effects mounting from inanition to mayhem. Perhaps we should conclude, as Eliot counselled us, that there are far worse things than settling for what we were born to. Indeed, the most poignant of all the reasons favouring that course inheres in culture itself. 'All these useless words', the Marxist Brownlow reflects bitterly,[42] as he clears his books from shelves that are no longer his. In this, he relays the ambivalence that persists from Hardy to Smith, the suspicion of educated men and women that the authority of culture – the presupposition of the genre – is itself inflated and flawed. Every bit as disinterested as it is said to be, culture is its own cruelly satirical reward, dangerous at worst, and in all not worth the candle.

8

The condition of culture novel as I have constructed its history here has been an English phenomenon – 'English' in its narrowest sense, that is, pertaining to England. A fuller, more adequate account would be comparative in design, searching across a range of literatures not only for further instances and other lineages but also different forms – variant or equivalent – of the genre, for while it is certain that these are there to be found, it seems unlikely at the same time that they will simply replicate the familiar features of the English line. Without such comparisons, indeed, the English genre itself is likely to remain under-defined and perhaps misconstrued altogether. It is only in the light of

---

42   Kureishi, *The Black Album*, p. 199.

methodical comparison that we can hope to leave familiarity behind and progress towards a more adequate rational construction of the object in its real individuality. Here then are some preliminary thoughts in conclusion: by no means that methodical comparison, but a first indication of the interest it might hold.

One probably unique example of the genre from the wider culture of the novel in English is Nabokov's *Lolita*, a dark parody of the language and culture of consumerism in the United States in the 1950s. From an earlier period in the American novel come the gallows-humorist Nathanael West's *A Cool Million*, again a work in which parody is a decisive resource, and his lacerating Hollywood fable, *The Day of the Locust*. With *Misery*, from the 1980s, Stephen King placed another fearsome exhibit in the gallery of popular literacy as horror.[43] These novels alone are strong evidence of a kindred American lineage, in the novelistic critique of mass culture, traceable over more than a half-century in the novel, and branching into cinema, in new work as well as adaptations.[44]

The artist-novel, or *Künstlerroman* as it is more often called, in recognition of its German type-site, can come close to the kind of general evaluation that the condition of culture novel proposes. David Leavitt's *Martin Bauman*, from 2000, is a case in point, with its critical articulation of a vocation (writing), a

---

43   The dates of publication are Nabokov, 1955; West, 1934 and 1939 respectively; King, 1987.

44   This is worth emphasizing, when the literary commentaries of recent decades have devoted so much attention to the contrary orientation: the appropriation of pop culture for the 'literary' novel, and narrative more generally. Contrastingly, Jonathan Franzen's *The Kraus Project* (2013), although in obvious respects a bestseller's perk, is notable as an act of affiliation to the high European tradition of *Kulturkritik*.

milieu (Manhattan's West Village) and a period (the years of the Reagan presidency and the metropolitan AIDS crisis). But the tension between art and the bourgeois everyday that is the defining problem of this genre is characteristically more narrowly framed, or so such examples as Joyce's *Portrait of the Artist as a Young Man* and Thomas Mann's *Tonio Kröger* would suggest. Alongside that novella and its companion-piece *Death in Venice* sit Mann's classic essay in cultural criticism, *Reflections of an Unpolitical Man*, and his great novel of ideas, *The Magic Mountain*. A satirical conspectus of European bourgeois culture in the last years of the Belle Epoque, that novel has visible affinities with the English tradition. Yet it is more various in its concerns than the simple designation 'condition of culture novel' suggests, and even in that aspect it diverges from the main English patterns in its basic symbolic conceit, the existential divorce between the timeless routines of the sanatorium in the Swiss Alps and the busy practical world of what its inmates call 'the flat-land', 5,000 metres below. A similar device structures the action and possibilities of another novel of culture from the German-language zone, Hermann Hesse's *The Glass Bead Game*. The only comparable cases in the English genre are *Brideshead* and *Orlando*, where the great houses embody alternative cultural orders. The valuations attached to these separated worlds vary significantly. Mann's 'flat-land' is the familiar world of interests and customary pieties but the sanatorium is hardly a virtuous antithesis: although it accommodates positive critical values, its intellectuality is ridiculous overall, often naive or sinister. Hesse's imagined province of intellect, Castalia, is in the end not enough to hold his protagonist, Joseph Knecht – for whom, nevertheless, the alternative of return to the ordinary world proves fatal. Brideshead's positives are real but historically residual, soon to be overwhelmed by mass vandalism. Only Orlando's house offers an ideal cultural time-space, the novel in itself having created the possibility, in virtue of its character as an unabashed exercise in the fantastic.[45]

What is absent in these German novels, as it is absent also in the American cases – and more or less radically edulcorated in the aristocratic fictions of Woolf and Waugh – is what stamps the English condition of culture novel: the preoccupation with class relations and, centrally, the matter of the working-class presence in culture.[46] Of course, narratives of class conflict have not been a peculiarity of the English, any more than novels of culture: *Jude the Obscure* came at the end of a ten-year span that produced three classic depictions of proletarian struggle on the European mainland: Zola's *Germinal*, Hauptmann's *Die Weber* and *Primo Maggio* by Edmondo De Amicis.[47] It is the combination of the

---

45   Mann's *Die Zauberberg* was first published in 1924, four years before *Orlando*; Hesse's *Das Glasperlenspiel* in 1943, two years before *Brideshead Revisited*. In more recent times, Bernhard Schlink's *The Reader* (1997; *Der Vorleser*, 1995) sounds an uncanny echo with the English history in its study of a young German woman whose determination to conceal her illiteracy leads her, quite matter-of-factly, into the wartime SS and eventual imprisonment as a war criminal – a variation on the familiar topos of *Kultur* and the death camps that, for all its national specificity, cannot but recall the story of Eunice Parchman.

46   Communism makes an appearance in *The Magic Mountain*, but only as a modality of the character Naptha's fanatical nihilism. The social reality of a modern working class is absent. This is noteworthy in a novel that was completed in Germany's revolutionary years – and in a country that for decades had been the symbolic head and heart of the international socialist workers movement.

47   Zola, 1885; Hauptmann, first performed 1892; *Primo Maggio*, written in immediate response to the murderous repression of a May Day demonstration in 1891, remained unpublished until 1980.

two that appears to distinguish the English tradition. And that, in its turn, must be seen in the light of a second comparison, this one temporal and internal to English (rather, British) literary history. The condition of culture novel in England was in one sense not an original departure at all. It was rather a modified resumption of a genre that had arisen half a century before *Jude*, in the mid-1840s, sustaining itself for a good two decades thereafter. This was the line running from Disraeli through Gaskell, Dickens, Kingsley and Eliot, familiar to readers of Raymond Williams as that of 'the industrial novel'.[48] *Sybil* (1845) and *North and South* (1855), to name just two of these novels, took as their defining concern the actual and emerging class relations of their time, which they described and evaluated in narratives of directly political and economic struggle. In a period when the fundamental terms of labour in the new industrial economy remained to be settled and after a decade in which the working class had massed under the revolutionary-democratic banner of the People's Charter, there was little scope for symbolic displacement. The fictional terms of resolution were correspondingly naive or ingenious, but there could be no escaping the reality of the crisis-ridden social relations they were set to work upon or the revolutionary storm-clouds they might magically disperse. Here, forty years ahead in time and bearing witness to Britain's priority in industrial-ization, are the historical equivalents of those French, German and Italian classics from the formative decades of the modern workers movement. (Indeed, Hauptmann's weavers belong to the 1840s, not his own time). The specificity of the English

---

48 Raymond Williams, *Culture and Society 1780–1950*, London, 1958, Pt. I, Ch. 5, 'The Industrial Novel'; and see also Williams, 'The Welsh Indus-trial Novel', *Problems in Materialism and Culture*, London, 1980, pp. 213–29.

condition of culture novel appears more clearly in the light of this two-part contrast. When *Germinal* was published, memories of the Paris Commune and its bloody repression were still vivid, and anti-parliamentary syndicalism was the prevailing sentiment in the French workers movement. Hauptmann's play appeared just as Germany's avowedly Marxist Social Democratic Party was emerging undefeated from more than a decade of illegality to enter the period of its greatest influence. In Italy, a comparable phase of repression was then beginning, in an ineffective attempt to counter the influence of socialism and anarchism among the working class. The temper and situation of the British working class, remade now from its earlier Chartist self, were of another kind. The new organizations that took shape towards the end of the nineteenth century were not even nominally socialist, let alone revolutionary. Liberalism still defined the social horizon of politics in the labour interest – and often the continuing electoral option too. As late as 1914, Europe's oldest industrial working class was trailing all its comparable neighbours in the development of independent political representation.[49]

These were not the unprecedented, radically uncertain conditions that had troubled the industrial novel into existence in the 1840s. They favoured another emphasis and another register of solicitude and anxiety: no longer the drama of collective struggle,

---

49   The oldest and just about the biggest, proportionally, bar Belgium, which could claim 45.1 per cent of employees engaged in industry, compared with Britain's 44.6 per cent. (The figures are for 1910 and 1911 respectively.) Labour's best electoral showing pre-1918 was 7.0 per cent; the corresponding figures for France, Italy and Germany were 16.8, 21.3 and 34.8 respectively. For more extensive comparative data, with details of sources, see Donald Sassoon, *One Hundred Years of Socialism: The West European Left in the Twentieth Century*, London, 1996, p. 10.

with its frontal collisions and predictable lurch into irrational violence, more the journey towards a better life, in a contrastingly individual endeavour, the ideally steady pace of political reform finding an apt figure in education and the will to culture. This was the general matrix of the English condition of culture novel – in which from the beginning, nevertheless, that peaceable liberal meliorism found a voice for its compulsive counter-imaginings. The ambivalence of the old genre persisted into the new one. With the solicitude came the anxiety and then the simpler negative dispositions of alienation, fear and revulsion. What in one perspective could be taken for progress in another seemed more like an unstoppable encroachment, the coming ascendancy of the earnest and the feather-brained, or culture's end.

There will be no end of such endings, in the tangible future, though they have become more diverse as new social subjects emerge from without and below to join or succeed the working class in its luckless, blundering, destructive transactions with culture. Culture as principle is an exclusive universal, a figure of discourse that produces and reproduces its own menacing other, an ideological power complicit with the social order that fosters the deformities it laments. At its most magnanimous, it rises to Vita Sackville-West's vision of Knole, the great house built on centuries of exploited labour, now to be opened to a spiritually ill-nourished public that might draw a little sustenance from their weekend visit. At its most anxious, the sacred places are Brideshead and Lowfield, and the queue has turned into a mob. The narrative curve of the condition of culture novel over the twentieth century has been from the first to the second of these states. There has been a good deal of variation from one novel to another, some of it important, but we should not exaggerate.

The constant of the genre overall has been fatalism, and a pessimism mounting to fantasies of catastrophe. There has been just enough diversity of social identification in this tradition to allow the thought that there might be other ways of imagining all those other lives and their historic potentials – but only just.

Index